BEST PRACTICES
for EFFECTIVE
SECONDARY
SCHOOL
COUNSELORS

Vision without action is merely a dream. Action without vision just passes the time. Vision with action can change the world.

—Joel Barker

BEST PRACTICES for EFFECTIVE SECONDARY SCHOOL COUNSELORS

Carla F. Shelton
Edward L. James

A Joint Publication

CORWIN
PRESS

AMERICAN
SCHOOL
COUNSELOR
ASSOCIATION

CORWIN PRESS
A Sage Publications Company
Thousand Oaks, California

For information:

Corwin Press
A Sage Publications Company
2455 Teller Road
Thousand Oaks, California 91320
www.corwinpress.com

Sage Publications Ltd.
1 Oliver's Yard
55 City Road
London EC1Y 1SP
United Kingdom

Sage Publications India Pvt. Ltd.
B-42, Panchsheel Enclave
Post Box 4109
New Delhi 110 017 India

Printed in the United States of America

Library of Congress Cataloging-in-Publication Data

Shelton, Carla F.
Best practices for effective secondary school counselors / by Carla F. Shelton and Edward L. James.
    p. cm.
Includes bibliographical references and index.
ISBN 1-4129-0449-8 (cloth) — ISBN 1-4129-0450-1 (pbk.)
    1. Counseling in secondary education—United States.
2. Student counselors—United States. I. James, Edward L. II. Title.
LB1620.5.S49 2005
373.14—dc22

                                                    2004014962

This book is printed on acid-free paper.

05 06 07 08 09 10 9 8 7 6 5 4 3 2 1

Acquisitions Editor:	Robert D. Clouse
Editorial Assistant:	Jingle Vea
Production Editors:	Julia Parnell, Diane Foster
Copy Editor:	Diana Breti
Typesetter:	C&M Digitals (P) Ltd.
Indexer:	Jean Casalengo
Cover Designer:	Michael Dubowe

Contents

Forms and Resources

FORMS

RESOURCES

Preface

Secondary school counselors across the United States confront a multitude of challenges in their journeys to prepare students to meet the demands of a global economy. The increase in the number of at-risk students, the increase in the level of educational attainment required for the modern work force, and the increase in college entrance requirements are a few of the issues that are prompting counselors to reevaluate their current school counseling programs. In the same manner, the age of high-stakes tests and teacher accountability has prompted school administrators to reevaluate their school's effectiveness, investigate various reform models, and develop appropriate restructuring plans that will assist school personnel to meet the needs of all students. Unfortunately, most of the federally recognized reform programs do not specifically address the issues or concerns of a school's counseling staff, but primarily focus on the school's climate, academic curriculum, instructional practices, and assessment approaches. A comprehensive counseling program is a critical component of a school's instructional program, and counselors play a vital role in school reform and school improvement. School counselors need assistance to develop effective practices and implement programs that are visionary by design and positively impact the school community if they are to continue to meet the ever-changing needs of diverse student populations and support the overall school improvement initiative.

According to the Indiana Department of Education (2002) a "best practice is a term that is used by many groups in society to describe 'what works' in a particular situation or environment. These practices can also be called research-based practice or scientifically-based practice if there is research to support its success in the field." In this book, we identify six Best Practices or strategies that profoundly affect and improve a school counselor's effectiveness in meeting the needs of stakeholders at the secondary school level. In addition, educational research pertaining to each practice is provided. The practices or strategies outlined focus on annual program evaluation, individual and schoolwide advisement, career education, transition, communication, and professional development for school counselors. They support the basic framework of the American School Counselor Association's National Model in theory and practice. We have designed specific programs and activities that reflect the various elements of the national model: foundation, delivery system, management systems, and accountability. Upon review of the literature, we found an increasing need for school counselors to create programs that are data driven and standards based. In this book, we guide counselors in designing and implementing visionary programs that assist students to develop realistic career and education plans, promote parent involvement and positive home relations, foster community and business partnerships, encourage students to complete challenging academic programs of study, and assist students with transitions to the next level of education or post-secondary experiences. The strategies for program evaluation, continuous improvement, and frameworks for specific programs will lay the foundation for a comprehensive school counseling system.

This book is a comprehensive resource designed to guide, assist, and support middle and high school counselors as they navigate through the program revitalization maze and move toward the integration of the American School Counseling Association's national model. Each chapter provides an overview of and research in support of a Best Practice, immediately preceded by a recommended program or programs that implement or apply the concept. Every program is described in detail to include goals, objectives, organizational steps, implementation procedures, and suggested materials. We provide numerous time-saving checklists, surveys, and forms that will assist the counselor to accomplish the multitude of tasks necessary to implement new programs. In addition, the book's chapters are written in an abbreviated format and can be reviewed in a matter of minutes.

Finally, this book is written from a practicing school counselor perspective and is designed for secondary school counselors who are striving to move their current programs from service-centered to program-centered. We have found that the academic programs of most schools are becoming standards-based and data-driven in order to ensure that students are meeting state and national standards. In the same light, the guidance and counseling program is an integral part of a school's academic programs and must mirror their efforts by establishing student competencies and implementing a process of continuous evaluation and improvement as an accountability measure. We provide the tools necessary to make this transformation. In addition, we contend that the academic, career, personal, and social development of students is not just the responsibility of the school counselor, but must be a joint effort that involves the entire school community. This philosophy is evidenced by the importance we have placed on involving all of the school's stakeholders in program development and implementation. The Best Practices can be tailored to fit the individual needs of most programs, and the simple strategies can easily be implemented by an individual school counselor or a school's counseling staff.

Acknowledgments

Carla would like to thank her daughters, Catherine, Lynsey, and Meredith, for their unconditional love and continuous encouragement throughout this endeavor. She thanks her husband, Drew, for his love, patience, and support as she follows her dreams.

Ed would like to thank his children, Ashley, Arica, and Aaron, for their encouragement and support. He would like to thank his wife, Lewana, for her patience and perseverance as he completes his thirty-sixth year in education.

Together, the authors would like to thank their school principal, Barry Hemphill, for instilling in them the desire to strive for excellence in the workplace and the importance of having vision when developing educational programs for students. In addition, the authors want to acknowledge the faculty and staff of Harlem High School for their relentless support of the School Counseling Program and their dedication to students.

Corwin Press gratefully acknowledges the contributions of the following people:

Gerald Monk
Author, Professor
Dept. of Psychology & Counseling
San Diego State University
San Diego, CA

Greg Brigman
Professor
College of Special Education
Florida Atlantic University
Boca Raton, FL

Barbara Blackburn
Secondary Level Vice President
American School Counselor
   Association (ASCA)
Greenbrier East High School
Lewisburg, WV

John M. Littrell
Professor
Counselor Education/Educational
   Leadership and Policy Studies
Iowa State University
Ames, IA

Judy Buchholz
School Counselor
O. W. Holmes Junior
   High School
Davis, CA

Karen D. Thompson
Assistant Professor
Dept. of Psychology & Counseling
Valdosta State University
Valdosta, GA

About the Authors

Carla F. Shelton, EdS, has fifteen years of experience in the education profession. Currently, she is a school counselor working with students in grades 9–12. She has taught students with disabilities in grades 2 through 12 in both resource and self-contained environments. Carla is certified in the areas of School Counseling (P–12), Educational Leadership and Supervision, Specific Learning Disabilities, Emotional/Behavior Disorders, Mildly Intellectual Disabilities, and Elementary Grades (P–8). Carla is the author of *The Exceptional Teacher's Handbook*.

During the past five years, she has been deeply involved with school reform and school improvement programs. Carla has expertise in developing and implementing programs designed to assist high school students in their academic and postsecondary endeavors; to bridge the gap among school, parents, and community; and to assist students in staying on track for graduation. She is knowledgeable in current instructional techniques and practices that support and enhance the high school curriculum. She has presented at the High Schools That Work Summer Conference, the National Tech Prep Conference, the Georgia School Counselor Conference, and the Association for Supervision and Curriculum Development Annual Conference. Carla's professional affiliations include the American School Counselor Association, Georgia School Counselor Association, National Tech Prep Network, and Professional Association of Georgia Educators. Finally, Carla's solid education background and broad-based educational experience are the foundation on which *Best Practices for Effective Secondary School Counselors* is built.

Edward L. James, EdS, has dedicated the last thirty-six years of his life to the education profession, with the last twenty-nine years dedicated solely to school counseling. He spent five years in the elementary and junior high setting and twenty-four years at the high school level. He received his degrees from Georgia Southern College. Edward is active in professional organizations both local and national. He is a member of the American School Counselor Association, Georgia School Counselor Association,

National Tech Prep Network, and Professional Association of Georgia Educators. Currently, Edward is a high school counselor who is committed to schoolwide advisement and middle to secondary school transition. He is skilled in developing needs assessments, program goals and objectives, and implementation strategies. Edward has served as a consultant for a number of schools in developing comprehensive adviser-advisee programs, and he is deeply involved with the *High Schools That Work* reform model created by the Southern Regional Education Board. Edward's knowledge, motivation, professionalism, and expertise make him an excellent co-author for *Best Practices for Effective Secondary School Counselors*.

As a writing team, the authors bring to this project solid professional credentials and expertise in the field of school counseling as well as the perspectives of classroom teachers and parents. Carla and Edward's shared beliefs, philosophies, and love for the profession of school counseling led to the writing of a book that epitomizes their common vision and charts a new course for high school counselors across the nation.

Best Practice 1

Use Data to Evaluate Program Effectiveness and Plan for Continuous Improvement

Best Practice 1: Use Data to Evaluate Program Effectiveness and Plan for Continuous Improvement

Secondary school counselors must annually evaluate their programs by using qualitative and quantitative data to measure the extent to which they are meeting the needs of stakeholders. A comprehensive evaluation will reveal a program's strengths, identify deficit areas, and facilitate counselors' efforts to develop strategic plans for program improvement. A thorough review of all available school data will enable counselors to answer the following questions formulated by Isaacs (2003):

- Are we effectively helping students achieve through our programs or individual interventions?
- Conversely, are we effectively identifying the barriers that need to be overcome for all or some students?
- How can we understand our population and thus design effective programs or interventions? And, once implemented, what difference did these make?
- If we have this knowledge, over what are we gaining power? (section 6, para. 1)

School counselors must enter the accountability arena and prove that their programs play a critical role in the academic development and achievement of students and support the overall school mission.

Counselors must become masters at collecting, analyzing, and using data to measure the success of strategies and interventions designed to assist students and the school community. According to Gysbers and Henderson (1994), "demonstrating accountability through the measured effectiveness of the delivery of the guidance program and the performance of the guidance staff helps ensure that students, parents, teachers, administrators, and the general public will continue to benefit from quality comprehensive guidance programs" (p. 362). In addition, the American School Counselor Association (2003) states, "accountability and evaluation of the school counseling program are absolute necessities" (p. 59). Although teachers and administrators have been forced to confront accountability issues for some time, this is a new challenge for school counselors. In order to meet this challenge, the counselor must perfect his or her skills in dealing with data, prove that the school counseling program is vital to the overall school mission, and demonstrate that his or her professional expertise is indispensable in the school reform process. The practice of using data to evaluate program effectiveness and to develop plans for program improvement is one that will not only increase the quality of the school counseling program but will enable the school counselor to meet the challenge and survive the accountability era.

In the pages that follow, we present a five-step process that is designed to assist the secondary school counselor in collecting, analyzing, and evaluating data for the purpose of program evaluation and improvement. The process requires the school counselor to (1) review his or her school district's written school counseling plan, (2) develop a school profile, (3) obtain stakeholders' perspectives, (4) create a self-evaluation instrument, and (5) formulate a school counseling program action plan. Each section in this chapter addresses a step in the evaluation process and contains procedures, checklists, and forms that will facilitate the school counselor's efforts to systematically evaluate his or her current program and devise an action plan for program improvement.

SECTION 1: REVIEW THE SCHOOL COUNSELING PLAN

The first step in the program evaluation process is to review the district's written school counseling plan. Typically, there are specific plans for elementary, middle, and high school grade levels that contain guidelines for school counselors and outline program requirements or expectations for each level. School counseling plans usually consist of a statement of beliefs, philosophy, rationale, mission or vision, program priorities, and a description of the school counselor's duties and responsibilities. Often, school counseling plans do not include standards, competencies, and indicators. However, these components are the compass that enables the school counselor to chart a course toward an effective counseling program. Standards, competencies, and indicators must be part of the overall school counseling plan in order for the counselor to conduct a program evaluation. As Gysbers and Henderson (1994) stated,

To conduct a program evaluation, program standards are required. Program standards are acknowledged measures of comparison or the criteria used to make judgments about the adequacy of the nature and structure of the program as well as the degree to which the program is in place. (p. 481)

The American School Counselor Association (ASCA; 2003) defines student *competencies* as the "specific knowledge, attitudes, and skills students should obtain or demonstrate as a result of participating in a school counseling program" (p. 14). An *indicator* describes how a standard will be achieved and the necessary evidence that will serve as documentation. We have included the ASCA National Standards to assist counselors whose current plans do not include this component (see Form 1.2). There is space on Form 1.2 to document all evidence that a designated standard has been achieved. The school counselor may obtain evidence from a variety of sources including student assessment results, student surveys, counselor observations, or postsecondary follow-up studies. We have included examples of qualitative and quantitative data in order to assist the school counselor to use a variety of data sources.

The following forms are found in this section:

Form 1.1 Program Evaluation Process

Form 1.2A –1.2I ASCA National Standards

Form 1.3 Qualitative and Quantitative Data Samples

SECTION 2: DEVELOP A SCHOOL PROFILE

A school profile will provide the counselor with current information about students and programs. The information found in the profile is broad in scope and will assist the school counselor to detect trends in student enrollment, attendance, and dropout rates, and to discover factors that have hindered or promoted the academic achievement of students. Dimmitt (2003) found that "identifying the factors that interfere with academic success is a crucial first step in the process of choosing interventions to address this issue, and the best way to gain an accurate picture of interfering factors is the use of data" (section 1, para. 2). A completed profile will allow data to be viewed in both an aggregated and disaggregated format. The school counselor must review the profile and add program goals and objectives to his or her comprehensive plan in order to address problematic areas. The school profile can be used to chart the yearly progress of students and the success of specific academic or counseling strategies. We recommend that counselors share the completed document with the school's stakeholders.

The following forms are found in this section:

Form 1.4A-1.4D High School Profile

Form 1.5A-1.5D Middle School Profile

SECTION 3: OBTAIN STAKEHOLDER PERSPECTIVES

Surveys are useful for obtaining stakeholders' perspectives on the effectiveness of a counseling program. We have found that a simple needs assessment survey can convey what the stakeholders want and expect from a school's counseling program. Forms 1.6 through 1.8 are student, parent, and teacher needs assessments that contain generic information and may be modified to meet the individual needs of most programs. We encourage school counselors to summarize and organize the results of each assessment and determine whether their current counseling program is meeting the needs of all stakeholders.

The following forms are found in this section:

Form 1.6 Student Needs Assessment

Form 1.7 Teacher Needs Assessment

Form 1.8 Parent Needs Assessment

SECTION 4: CREATE A SELF-EVALUATION INSTRUMENT

We have developed an annual self-evaluation instrument for school counselors. It is based on the Utah State Office of Education (2003) Comprehensive Guidance Program Model and has been modified to include indicators that can be applied to most school counselors and their programs. The self-evaluation survey may be completed by the individual counselor or by the counseling staff.

The following forms are found in this section:

Form 1.9 A Self-Evaluation Instrument for the School Counselor

SECTION 5: FORMULATE A COUNSELING PROGRAM ACTION PLAN

Once all data have been collected and analyzed, the school counselor must formulate an improvement plan for the counseling department. We suggest involving the counseling advisory council in the development of the plan. An advisory council should represent all stakeholders, be kept to a manageable size, and meet on a monthly basis. School counselors should have an agenda for each meeting and designate an individual to take minutes. The counseling improvement plan should be composed of goal statements, current performance levels, benchmarks for improvement, performance indicators, assessment tools, and strategies for implementation. In addition, the plan must support the overall school mission.

The following forms are found in this section:

Form 1.10 School Counseling Program Action Plan

FORM 1.1

Program Evaluation Process

STEPS	TASKS
1. Review all components of the district's written school counseling plan.	The school counselor will review: beliefs and philosophy rationale mission or vision statement program priorities counselor duties and responsibilities program standards and benchmarks
2. Develop a comprehensive school profile.	The school counselor will collect the following information in order to develop a comprehensive school profile: student demographics student test data student attendance student dropouts student graduation statistics student diploma completion student extracurricular activities student discipline information student placement in special programs student postsecondary activities
3. Obtain stakeholders' perspectives.	The school counselor will conduct needs assessments in order to obtain stakeholder perspectives: student surveys parent surveys teacher surveys
4. Create a self-evaluation instrument.	The school counselor will develop a self-evaluation instrument that includes the following areas: professional development/professional responsibilities structural components delivery system additional programs or initiatives
5. Formulate a school counseling program action plan.	The school counselor will complete the following activities in order to formulate a school counseling program action plan: analyze and summarize data organize a guidance advisory council develop a school counseling action plan

FORM 1.2A

ASCA National Standards

Academic Development: Standard A

STANDARDS	COMPETENCIES	INDICATORS	EVIDENCE
Standard A Students will acquire the attitudes, knowledge, and skills that contribute to effective learning in school and across the life span.	A:A1 Improve Academic Self-Concept	A:A1.1 Articulate feelings of competence and confidence as learners A:A1.2 Display a positive interest in learning A:A1.3 Take pride in work and achievement A:A1.4 Accept mistakes as essential to the learning process A:A1.5 Identify attitudes and behaviors that lead to successful learning	
	A:A2 Acquire Skills for Improving Learning	A:A2.1 Apply time management and task management skills A:A2.2 Demonstrate how effort and persistence positively affect learning A:A2.3 Use communications skills to know when and how to ask for help when needed A:A2.4 Apply knowledge and learning styles to positively influence school performance	
	A:A3 Achieve School Success	A:A3.1 Take responsibility for their actions A:A3.2 Demonstrate the ability to work independently, as well as the ability to work cooperatively with other students A:A3.3 Develop a broad range of interests and abilities A:A3.4 Demonstrate dependability, productivity, and initiative A:A3.5 Share knowledge	

FORM 1.2B

ASCA National Standards

Academic Development: Standard B

STANDARDS	COMPETENCIES	INDICATORS	EVIDENCE
Standard B Students will complete school with the academic preparation essential to choose from a wide range of substantial postsecondary options, including college.	A:B1 Improve Learning	A:B1.1 Demonstrate the motivation to achieve individual potential A:B1.2 Learn and apply critical-thinking skills A:B1.3 Apply the study skills necessary for academic success at each level A:B1.4 Seek information and support from faculty, staff, family, and peers A:B1.5 Organize and apply academic information from a variety of sources A:B1.6 Use knowledge of learning styles to positively influence school performance A:B1.7 Become a self-directed and independent learner	
	A:B2 Plan to Achieve Goals	A:B2.1 Establish challenging academic goals in elementary, middle/junior high, and high school A:B2.2 Use assessment results in educational planning A:B2.3 Develop and implement annual plan of study to maximize academic ability and achievement A:B2.4 Apply knowledge of aptitudes and interests to goal setting A:B2.5 Use problem-solving and decision-making skills to assess progress toward educational goals A:B2.6 Understand the relationship between classroom performance and success in school A:B2.7 Identify postsecondary options consistent with interests, achievement, aptitude, and abilities	

FORM 1.2C

ASCA National Standards

Academic Development: Standard C

STANDARDS	COMPETENCIES	INDICATORS	EVIDENCE
Standard C Students will understand the relationship of academics to the world of work and to life at home and in the community.	A:C1 Relate School to Life Experiences	A:C1.1 Demonstrate the ability to balance school, studies, extracurricular activities, leisure time, and family life A:C1.2 Seek co-curricular and community experiences to enhance the school experience A:C1.3 Understand the relationship between learning and work A:C1.4 Demonstrate an understanding of the value of lifelong learning as essential to seeking, obtaining, and maintaining life goals A:C1.5 Understand that school success is the preparation to make the transition from student to community member A:C1.6 Understand how school success and academic achievement enhance future career and vocational opportunities	

FORM 1.2D

ASCA National Standards

Career Development: Standard A

STANDARDS	COMPETENCIES	INDICATORS	EVIDENCE
Standard A Students will acquire the skills to investigate the world of work in relation to knowledge of self and to make informed career decisions.	C:A1 Develop Career Awareness	C:A1.1 Develop skills to locate, evaluate, and interpret career information C:A1.2 Learn about the variety of traditional and nontraditional occupations C:A1.3 Develop an awareness of personal abilities, skills, interests, and motivations C:A1.4 Learn how to interact and work cooperatively in teams C:A1.5 Learn to make decisions C:A1.6 Learn how to set goals C:A1.7 Understand the importance of planning C:A1.8 Pursue and develop competency in areas of interest C:A1.9 Develop hobbies and vocational interests C:A1.10 Balance between work and leisure time	
	C:A2 Develop Employment Readiness	C:A2.1 Acquire employability skills such as teamwork, problem-solving, and organizational skills C:A2.2 Apply job readiness skills to seek employment opportunities C:A2.3 Demonstrate knowledge about the changing workplace C:A2.4 Learn about the rights and responsibilities of employers and employees C:A2.5 Learn to respect individual uniqueness in the workplace C:A2.6 Learn how to write a résumé C:A2.7 Develop a positive attitude toward work and learning C:A2.8 Understand the importance of responsibility, dependability, punctuality, integrity, and effort in the workplace C:A2.9 Utilize time and task management skills	

FORM 1.2E

ASCA National Standards

Career Development: Standard B

STANDARDS	COMPETENCIES	INDICATORS	EVIDENCE
Standard B Students will employ strategies to achieve future career goals with success and satisfaction.	C:B1 Acquire Career Information	C:B1.1 Apply decision-making skills to career planning, course selection, and career transition C:B1.2 Identify personal skills, interests, and abilities and relate them to current career choice C:B1.3 Demonstrate knowledge of the career-planning process C:B1.4 Know the various ways in which occupations can be classified C:B1.5 Use research and information resources to obtain career information C:B1.6 Learn to use the Internet to access career planning information C:B1.7 Describe traditional and nontraditional career choices and how they relate to career choice C:B1.8 Understand how changing economic and societal needs influence employment trends and future training	
	C:B2 Identify Career Goals	C:B2.1 Demonstrate awareness of the education and training needed to achieve career goals C:B2.2 Assess and modify their educational plan to support career C:B2.3 Use employability and job readiness skills in internship, mentoring, shadowing, and/or other work experience C:B2.4 Select course work that is related to career interests C:B2.5 Maintain a career-planning portfolio	

FORM 1.2F

ASCA National Standards

Career Development: Standard C

STANDARDS	COMPETENCIES	INDICATORS	EVIDENCE
Standard C Students will understand the relationship between personal qualities, education, training, and the world of work.	C:C1 Acquire Knowledge to Achieve Career Goals	C:C1.1 Understand the relationship between educational achievement and career success C:C1.2 Explain how work can help to achieve personal success and satisfaction C:C1.3 Identify personal preferences and interests influencing career choice and success C:C1.4 Understand that the changing workplace requires lifelong learning and acquiring new skills C:C1.5 Describe the effect of work on lifestyle C:C1.6 Understand the importance of equity and access in career choice C:C1.7 Understand that work is an important and satisfying means of personal expression	
	C:C2 Apply Skills to Achieve Career Goals	C:C2.1 Demonstrate how interests, abilities, and achievement relate to achieving personal, social, educational, and career goals C:C2.2 Learn how to use conflict management skills with peers and adults C:C2.3 Learn to work cooperatively with others as a team member C:C2.4 Apply academic and employment readiness skills in work-based learning situations such as internships, shadowing, and/or mentoring experiences	

FORM 1.2G

ASCA National Standards

Personal/Social: Standard A

STANDARDS	COMPETENCIES	INDICATORS	EVIDENCE
Standard A Students will acquire the knowledge, attitudes, and interpersonal skills to help them understand and respect self and others.	PS:A1 Acquire Self-Knowledge	PS:A1.1 Develop positive attitudes toward self as a unique and worthy person PS:A1.2 Identify values, attitudes, and beliefs PS:A1.3 Learn the goal-setting process PS:A1.4 Understand change is a part of growth PS:A1.5 Identify and express feelings PS:A1.6 Distinguish between appropriate and inappropriate behavior PS:A1.7 Recognize personal boundaries, rights, and privacy needs PS:A1.8 Understand the need for self-control and how to practice it PS:A1.9 Demonstrate cooperative behavior in groups PS:A1.10 Identify personal strengths and assets PS:A1.11 Identify and discuss changing personal and social roles PS:A1.12 Identify and recognize changing family roles	
	PS:A2 Acquire Interpersonal Skills	PS:A2.1 Recognize that everyone has rights and responsibilities PS:A2.2 Respect alternative points of view PS:A2.3 Recognize, accept, respect, and appreciate individual differences PS:A2.4 Recognize, accept, and appreciate ethnic and cultural diversity PS:A2.5 Recognize and respect differences in various family configurations PS:A2.6 Use effective communication skills PS:A2.7 Know that communication involves speaking, listening, and nonverbal behavior PS:A2.8 Learn how to make and keep friends	

FORM 1.2H

ASCA National Standards

Personal/Social: Standard B

STANDARDS	COMPETENCIES	INDICATORS	EVIDENCE
Standard B Students will make decisions, set goals, and take necessary action to achieve goals.	PS:B1 Self-Knowledge Application	PS:B1.1 Use a decision-making and problem-solving model PS:B1.2 Understand consequences of decisions and choices PS:B1.3 Identify alternative solutions to a problem PS:B1.4 Develop effective coping skills for dealing with problems PS:B1.5 Demonstrate when, where, and how to seek help for solving problems and making decisions PS:B1.6 Know how to apply conflict resolution skills PS:B1.7 Demonstrate a respect and appreciation for individual and cultural differences PS:B1.8 Know when peer pressure is influencing a decision PS:B1.9 Identify long- and short-term goals PS:B1.10 Identify alternative ways to achieve goals PS:B1.11 Use persistence and perseverance in acquiring knowledge and skills PS:B1.12 Develop an action plan to set and achieve realistic goals	

FORM 1.2I

ASCA National Standards

Personal/Social: Standard C

STANDARDS	COMPETENCIES	INDICATORS	EVIDENCE
Standard C Students will understand safety and survival skills.	PS:C1 Acquire Personal Safety Skills	PS:C1.1 Demonstrate knowledge of personal information (i.e., telephone number, home address, emergency contact) PS:C1.2 Learn about the relationship between rules, laws, safety, and the protection of rights of the individual PS:C1.3 Learn about the differences between appropriate and inappropriate physical contact PS:C1.4 Demonstrate the ability to set boundaries, rights, and personal privacy PS:C1.5 Differentiate between situations requiring peer support and situations requiring adult professional help PS:C1.6 Identify resource people in the school and community, and know how to seek their help PS:C1.7 Apply effective problem-solving and decision-making skills to make safe and healthy choices PS:C1.8 Learn about the emotional and physical dangers of substance use and abuse PS:C1.9 Learn how to cope with peer pressure PS:C1.10 Learn techniques for managing stress and conflict PS:C1.11 Learn coping skills for managing life events	

Reprinted from American School Counselor Association, 2003, pp. 81–86.

FORM 1.3

Qualitative and Quantitative Data Samples

QUALITATIVE DATA	*QUANTITATIVE DATA*
Interviews	Standardized Test Results (e.g., PSAT, SAT, ACT, High School Graduation)
Direct Observations	Discipline Referrals
Surveys	Dropout Rate
Counselor Logs	Attendance Rate
Anecdotal Records	Promotion and Retention Rate
Case Studies	Graduation Completion Rate
Other:	Other:

FORM 1.4A

High School Profile

School Year: _____

	African Am.		Asian		Caucasian		Hispanic		Native Am.		Other		Total
Enrollment	M	F	M	F	M	F	M	F	M	F	M	F	Total
Grade 9													
Grade 10													
Grade 11													
Grade 12													
Total Students Enrollment													
Promoted by Grade	M	F	M	F	M	F	M	F	M	F	M	F	Total
Grade 9													
Grade 10													
Grade 11													
Grade 12													
Total Students Promoted													
Dropout by Grade	M	F	M	F	M	F	M	F	M	F	M	F	Total
Grade 9													
Grade 10													
Grade 11													
Grade 12													
Total Student Dropout													

FORM 1.4B

High School Profile

School Year: _____

General Student Information	African Am.		Asian		Caucasian		Hispanic		Native Am.		Other		
	M	F	M	F	M	F	M	F	M	F	M	F	Total
Student Average Daily Attendance													
Students on Free or Reduced Lunch													
Students Participating in Extracurricular Activities													
Students Participating in a Gifted Education Program													
Students Enrolled in a Remedial Education Program													
Students Enrolled in the College Preparatory Program of Study													
Students Enrolled in the Career Technical Program of Study													

FORM 1.4B

High School Profile (Continued)

General Student Information	African Am.		Asian		Caucasian		Hispanic		Native Am.		Other		Total
	M	F	M	F	M	F	M	F	M	F	M	F	
Students Enrolled in at Least 1 Advanced Placement Course													
Students Enrolled in at Least 2 Advanced Placement Courses													
Students Enrolled in at Least 3 Advanced Placement Courses													
Number of Graduates Attending Postsecondary Institutions													
Number of Graduates Entering the Work Force													

FORM 1.4C

High School Profile

School Year: _____

Student Performance Information	African Am.		Asian		Caucasian		Hispanic		Native Am.		Other		Total
	M	F	M	F	M	F	M	F	M	F	M	F	
Number of Students Scoring a "3" or Higher on at Least 1 Advanced Placement Exam													
Number of Students Taking the SAT													
Average SAT Score													
Average Verbal Score													
Average Math Score													
Average Writing Score													
Number of Students Taking the ACT													
Percentage of Students Passing the State Writing Assessment													
Percentage of Students Passing the State Language Arts Assessment													

FORM 1.4C

High School Profile (Continued)

Student Performance Information	African Am.		Asian		Caucasian		Hispanic		Native Am.		Other		Total
	M	F	M	F	M	F	M	F	M	F	M	F	
Percentage of Students Passing the State Mathematics Assessment													
Percentage of Students Passing the State Science Assessment													
Percentage of Students Passing the State Social Studies Assessment													
Percentage of Students Passing Algebra I													
Percentage of Students Passing Geometry													
Percentage of Students Passing Algebra II													
Percentage of Students Passing World History													
Percentage of Students Passing U.S. History													
Percentage of Students Passing Citizenship													

FORM 1.4C

High School Profile (Continued)

Student Performance Information	African Am.		Asian		Caucasian		Hispanic		Native Am.		Other		Total
	M	F	M	F	M	F	M	F	M	F	M	F	
Percentage of Students Passing English I													
Percentage of Students Passing English II													
Percentage of Students Passing English III													
Percentage of Students Passing English IV													
Percentage of Students Passing Spanish I													
Percentage of Students Passing Spanish II													
Percentage of Students Passing German I													
Percentage of Students Passing German II													
Percentage of Students Passing French I													
Percentage of Students Passing French II													

FORM 1.4D

High School Profile

School Year: _____

Discipline	African Am.		Asian		Caucasian		Hispanic		Native Am.		Other	
	M	F	M	F	M	F	M	F	M	F	M	F	Total
Number of Students Assigned In-School Suspension													
Number of Students Assigned Out-of-School Suspension													
Number of Students Assigned Long-Term Suspension													
Additional Information	M	F	M	F	M	F	M	F	M	F	M	F	Total

FORM 1.5A

Middle School Profile

School Year: _____

Enrollment	African Am.		Asian		Caucasian		Hispanic		Native Am.		Other		Total
	M	F	M	F	M	F	M	F	M	F	M	F	
Grade 6													
Grade 7													
Grade 8													
Total Student Enrollment													
Promoted by Grade	M	F	M	F	M	F	M	F	M	F	M	F	Total
Grade 6													
Grade 7													
Grade 8													
Dropouts by Grade	M	F	M	F	M	F	M	F	M	F	M	F	Total
Grade 6													
Grade 7													
Grade 8													

FORM 1.5B

Middle School Profile

School Year: _____

General Student Information	African Am.		Asian		Caucasian		Hispanic		Native Am.		Other		Total
	M	F	M	F	M	F	M	F	M	F	M	F	Total
Student Average Daily Attendance													
Students on Free or Reduced Lunch													
Students Participating in Extracurricular Activities													
Students Participating in Before or Afterschool Tutoring Program													
Students Participating in a Gifted Education Program													
Students Enrolled in the Title I Program													
Students Enrolled in a Special Education Program													

Discipline Information	M	F	M	F	M	F	M	F	M	F	M	F	Total
Number of Students Assigned In-School Suspension													
Number of Students Assigned Out-of-School Suspension													
Number of Students Assigned Long-Term Suspension													

FORM 1.5C

Middle School Profile

School Year: _____

Student Assessment Information	African Am.		Asian		Caucasian		Hispanic		Native Am.		Other		Total
	M	F	M	F	M	F	M	F	M	F	M	F	
Percentage of Students Passing the State Writing Assessment													
Percentage of Students Passing the State Language Arts Assessment													
Percentage of Students Passing the State Mathematics Assessment													
Percentage of Students Passing the State Science Assessment													
Percentage of Students Passing the State Social Studies Assessment													
Percentage of Students Passing Algebra I													
Percentage of Students Passing English I													
Percentage of Students Passing Spanish I													
Number of Students Taking the SAT for the Duke University Talent Program													

FORM 1.5D

Middle School Profile

School Year: _____

Additional Information	African Am.		Asian		Caucasian		Hispanic		Native Am.		Other		Total
	M	F	M	F	M	F	M	F	M	F	M	F	

FORM 1.6

Student Needs Assessment

School Year: _____

Directions: The school Counseling Department would appreciate your assistance with an important project designed to help us provide the best services to our students. As a first step in our project, we are asking you to complete the questionnaire below. PLEASE CHECK EACH STATEMENT THAT IS IMPORTANT TO YOU. Thank you!

Circle your grade: 6   7   8   9   10   11   12

Check one: Male _____   Female _____

I would like to know how to:

_____ 1. Solve problems and make good decisions

_____ 2. Set goals for myself and carry them out

_____ 3. Manage my time and tasks better

_____ 4. Cope with pressures from school, home, friends, and myself

_____ 5. Ask for what I want in an acceptable and assertive manner

_____ 6. Get along with others (teachers, parents, friends)

_____ 7. Accept criticism better

_____ 8. Better understand people who are different

_____ 9. Better understand myself

_____ 10. Get help when I need it

_____ 11. Be more comfortable about speaking up in class (asking questions, answering questions, participating in group activities)

_____ 12. Communicate better with peers

_____ 13. Resolve conflict with others

_____ 14. Better understand my abilities, interests, and aptitudes

_____ 15. Improve my study skills and test-taking skills

_____ 16. Select the most appropriate courses in school

_____ 17. Explore career choices

_____ 18. Write a résumé

_____ 19. Acquire and improve job interview skills

_____ 20. Develop and manage my career portfolio

_____ 21. Get part-time employment

_____ 22. Obtain information about educational options after high school

_____ 23. Get financial aid information for postsecondary education

_____ 24. Better understand college entrance requirements

FORM 1.6

Student Needs Assessment (Continued)

What are some other ways in which the counselors can help you?

_____

_____

_____

_____

_____

_____

_____

Please use the space below to record your ideas.

_____

_____

_____

_____

_____

_____

_____

_____

FORM 1.7

Teacher Needs Assessment

School Year: _____

Directions: The school Counseling Department would like your assistance in determining priorities for students and faculty. By responding to this survey, you will provide information helpful to our counseling activities and programs.

Please indicate how much you value each counselor function according to the following scale. For items A–J, rate for value to students and for items K–O, rate for value to faculty.

Circle the appropriate number.

1-No Importance	2-Little Importance	3-Important	4-Very Important	5-Extremely Important

A. <u>Individual Counseling:</u>   1   2   3   4   5

For personal or school-related problems.

B. <u>Group Counseling:</u>   1   2   3   4   5

Small groups of a developmental preventative nature. Groups usually meet 6–12 times.

C. <u>Peer Assistance:</u>   1   2   3   4   5

Enlisting selected students to work with students who need additional guidance and support.

D. <u>Parent Consultation:</u>   1   2   3   4   5

Consult with parents about student concerns and provide resource information.

E. <u>Crisis Intervention:</u>   1   2   3   4   5

Provide immediate services for students or teachers as needed in crisis situations.

F. <u>Orientation Programs:</u>   1   2   3   4   5

Provide orientation for all new students.

G. <u>Skills Training:</u>   1   2   3   4   5

Small group training in communication skills, assertiveness, study skills, decision making, conflict management, leadership skills, etc.

H. <u>Educational Planning:</u>   1   2   3   4   5

Counsel students regarding academic concerns and/or course selection.

I. <u>Postsecondary Planning:</u>   1   2   3   4   5

Provide counseling and information regarding postsecondary training/educational opportunities.

J. <u>Career Planning:</u>   1   2   3   4   5

Assist students in self-understanding (interests, abilities, aptitudes, vocational goals) and exploration of career information.

FORM 1.7

Teacher Needs Assessment (Continued)

K. Teacher Consultation: 1   2   3   4   5

Consult with teachers regarding curriculum needs of students, behavioral concerns, and/or students with disabilities.

L. Referrals: 1   2   3   4   5

Utilize school community resources such as social workers, school psychologists, and vocational rehabilitation specialists to provide services for students with disabilities.

M. Classroom Guidance: 1   2   3   4   5

Lead guidance units on educational planning, career information, and/or personal and social skills.

N. Department Liaison: 1   2   3   4   5

Serve as liaisons with all departments to foster interaction on common concerns.

O. Professional Development: 1   2   3   4   5

Provide learning experiences for staff members on topics of interest such as stress management, assertiveness, conflict resolution, communication skills, and/or Teacher Effectiveness Training.

Please write below or use a separate sheet of paper to comment on the activities listed in this assessment and/or suggest other ways our counseling department can assist you, our students, or the school.

_____

_____

_____

_____

_____

_____

Thank you for your help and participation!

FORM 1.8

Parent Needs Assessment

School Year: _____

Directions: The School Counseling Department would like your assistance in determining programs and services that would best meet the needs of parents. Please complete the survey below and check each statement that is important to you or your child. Thank you for your continued support!

Circle your son's or daughter's current grade: 6 7 8 9 10 11 12

Check one: Male _____   Female _____

Circle the appropriate number.

1-No Importance	2-Little Importance	3-Important	4-Very Important	5-Extremely Important

My son or daughter is in need of

A. Individual Counseling: 1   2   3   4   5

   For personal or school-related problems.

B. Group Counseling: 1   2   3   4   5

   Small groups of a developmental preventative nature. Groups usually meet 6-12 times.

C. Skills Training: 1   2   3   4   5

   Small-group training in communication skills, assertiveness, study skills, decision making, conflict management, leadership skills, etc.

D. Academic Services: 1   2   3   4   5

   Tutorial services and/or SAT/ACT prep classes.

E. Orientation/Transition Programs: 1   2   3   4   5

   Orientation for all new students and parents.

F. Educational Planning: 1   2   3   4   5

   Counseling regarding academic concerns and/or course selection.

G. Career Planning: 1   2   3   4   5

   Assistance in self-understanding (interests, abilities, aptitudes, vocational goals) and exploration of career information.

FORM 1.8

Parent Needs Assessment (Continued)

As a parent, I am in need of

H. <u>Parent Consultation:</u>   1   2   3   4   5

    Consultation about student concerns and resource information.

I. <u>Orientation Programs:</u>   1   2   3   4   5

    Orientation for all new students and parents.

J. <u>Parent Workshops:</u>   1   2   3   4   5

    Programs for parents to address specific issues or topics such as *Dealing With Difficult Teens, How to Help Students With Homework, What to Expect During the Middle School Years.*

K. <u>Postsecondary Planning:</u>   1   2   3   4   5

    Counseling and information regarding postsecondary training, educational opportunities, and financial aid.

L. <u>Referrals:</u>   1   2   3   4   5

    Referrals to community resources.

Please write below or use a separate sheet of paper to comment on the activities listed in this survey and/or suggest other ways our Counseling Department can assist you, our students, or the school.

_____

_____

_____

_____

_____

_____

Thank you for your help and participation!

FORM 1.9A

A Self-Evaluation Instrument for the School Counselor

School Year:_____

INDICATORS   PERFORMANCE LEVELS

PROFESSIONAL DEVELOPMENT/ PROFESSIONAL RESPONSIBILITIES	EXEMPLARY	SATISFACTORY	NEEDS IMPROVEMENT
The school counselor participates in professional development activities in order to stay current in his or her field.			
The school counselor attends district, state, and/or national conferences on a yearly basis.			
The school counselor is a member of and participates in professional organizations.			
The school counselor clearly understands state and federal laws regarding student records and information (e.g., FERPA).			
The school counselor maintains a log of all student, parent, faculty, and community contacts. A summary report of all activity is completed on a monthly basis.			
The school counselor formulates an advisory committee each school year composed of representatives of the school's stakeholders. The committee supports and assists the school counselor to develop specific guidelines and goals based on an assessment of students' needs and other measurable data.			
The school counselor participates in revising and updating the school counseling program's action plan each year.			

FORM 1.9B

A Self-Evaluation Instrument for the School Counselor

STRUCTURAL COMPONENTS	EXEMPLARY	SATISFACTORY	NEEDS IMPROVEMENT
The school counselor ensures that the counseling office has an inviting outer reception area.			
The school counselor assists in developing a yearly budget that adequately supports all programs and services conducted by the department.			
The school counselor has the skills necessary to effectively utilize technology in the workplace.			
The school counselor extends the work day in order to meet the needs of students and parents.			
The middle school counselor annually meets with feeder elementary school counselors to coordinate the transition of rising sixth-grade students.			
The high school counselor annually meets with feeder middle school counselors to coordinate the transition of rising ninth-grade students.			
The school counselor creates and maintains a Web page on the school's Web site.			
The school counselor uses his or her Web page to communicate information to the school community.			
The school counselor assists in developing a yearly calendar of events.			

FORM 1.9C

A Self-Evaluation Instrument for the School Counselor

DELIVERY SYSTEM -Individual Student Planning-	EXEMPLARY	SATISFACTORY	NEEDS IMPROVEMENT
The school counselor spends at least eighty percent of his or her time providing direct services to students.			
The school counselor conducts individual advisement sessions with each student on his or her caseload on an annual basis, in order to discuss program planning and review the student's progress toward plan completion.			
The school counselor invites each parent to attend an individual advisement session with his or her child on an annual basis.			
The school counselor conducts programs and activities that address issues identified from previously administered needs assessments.			
The school counselor uses needs assessments and other school data to prioritize strategies and interventions.			
DELIVERY SYSTEM -Response Services-	EXEMPLARY	SATISFACTORY	NEEDS IMPROVEMENT
The school counselor is available and makes timely responses to students, parents, and faculty.			
The school counselor effectively follows up with students or others as required following responsive services contact.			
The school counselor effectively collaborates with school, community, and family resources.			
The school counselor has assisted with the development of a crisis response plan. The plan is available for immediate implementation.			

37

FORM 1.9C

A Self-Evaluation Instrument for the School Counselor (Continued)

DELIVERY SYSTEM -Response Services-	EXEMPLARY	SATISFACTORY	NEEDS IMPROVEMENT
The school counselor provides continuous, effective groups and classes to deal with ongoing student issues (e.g., grief, divorce, transitions, violence).			
The school counselor exchanges information with feeder school counselors in an effort to support responsive services and student success.			

DELIVERY SYSTEM -Guidance Curriculum-	EXEMPLARY	SATISFACTORY	NEEDS IMPROVEMENT
The school counselor conducts classroom guidance activities throughout the school year.			
The school counselor teaches study and time-management skills.			
The school counselor reviews and explains specific standardized tests (e.g., PSAT, SAT, ACT, AP).			
The school counselor reviews and explains specific state tests (e.g., high school graduation tests).			
The school counselor provides comprehensive career exploration and development activities.			
The school counselor provides a wide variety of information and resources (e.g., interest inventories, computer delivery systems, business and community organizations) to promote career development, exploration, and job shadowing opportunities for all students.			
The school counselor assists students to develop job seeking skills and post–high school placement.			

FORM 1.9D

A Self-Evaluation Instrument for the School Counselor

ADDITIONAL PROGRAMS	EXEMPLARY	SATISFACTORY	NEEDS IMPROVEMENT
The school counselor assists in developing and implementing orientation programs for feeder schools.			
The school counselor conducts parent workshops based on the completed parent needs surveys or assessments.			
The school counselor plans and conducts field trips to postsecondary institutions.			
The school counselor assists in organizing a career day each school year.			
The school counselor assists in organizing a college day each school year.			
The school counselor assists in organizing an advisement program.			
The school counselor assists in organizing standardized test prep classes (e.g., SAT, ACT, AP).			

Adapted from Utah State Office of Education, 2003, pp. 6–31.

FORM 1.10

School Counseling Program Action Plan

School Year: _____

Directions: The School Counseling Program Action Plan is designed to assist the counseling staff in setting priorities for program improvement. The Action Plan should be completed by the entire counseling department upon review of all program assessment data and the school profile.

GOAL STATEMENT	
CURRENT	
PERFORMANCE LEVEL	
BENCHMARKS FOR IMPROVEMENT	
PERFORMANCE INDICATORS	
ASSESSMENT TOOLS	
STRATEGIES FOR IMPLEMENTATION	

Comments: _____

_____

_____

_____

Best Practice 2

Design and Implement a Comprehensive Advisement System

Best Practice 2: Design and Implement a Comprehensive Advisement System

School counselors at the middle and high school levels are confronting the increased needs of diverse student populations, high school graduation requirements, the rising rigor of college entrance requirements, and entry-level skills necessary for the modern workforce. Students must possess solid academic and career plans in order to gain access to post-secondary education and employment opportunities. Traditionally, school counselors have had the sole responsibility for assisting students to develop and monitor these plans; however, counselors must make a paradigm shift and realize that this task is the shared responsibility of the school community. Counselors must design and implement strategies that involve all stakeholders in efforts to facilitate the educational, career, personal, and social development of students. A comprehensive advisement system will increase student contact with the faculty and staff and ensure students' education and career planning are monitored by school personnel. Advisement systems enhance the overall school climate, build strong bridges between home and school, and facilitate students' transitions to high school and postsecondary experiences. Parents, teachers, and staff must encourage students to complete challenging school courses, pursue areas of concentration in career and technical areas, and set realistic educational and career goals in order to be successful. Dr. Gene Bottoms of the Southern Regional Education Board (SREB) specifically outlines in the *High Schools That Work* reform model the importance of implementing a guidance and advisement system: "Schools can improve student achievement by increasing the amount of time available for students to talk with counselors and teachers about completing a challenging program of study. Adult advisers are proof that the school cares about its students" (Bottoms, Han, & Presson, 2003, p. 26). A comprehensive advisement system provides numerous opportunities for a school's faculty and staff to get to know students on a personal level and view them as total beings with real interests, hopes, and dreams. In addition, this system provides students with a sense of belonging and an understanding that at least one adult in the school has an interest in whether he or she succeeds or fails. A successful, comprehensive advisement system has three components: a schoolwide advisement program, an individual advisement program, and a rising ninth-grade advisement program.

In the pages that follow, we provide the goals, objectives, organizational steps, session formats, required materials, and lessons learned for each component of a comprehensive advisement system. The chapter is divided into three major sections with each section targeting a specific advisement program. We highly recommend that the school counselor and counseling staff form a committee to review each program and modify the concepts to meet the needs of the current student population. All three advisement programs are meant to enhance a school counseling program's delivery system and facilitate the academic, career, and personal/social development of middle and high school students.

SECTION 1: A SCHOOLWIDE ADVISEMENT PROGRAM

A schoolwide advisement program is a total school effort involving all certified school personnel serving as advisers. Advisers are responsible for mentoring a specific group of students and remain with the same group until graduation. During each advisement session, advisers conduct mini-lessons on designated topics and meet with students individually to discuss their last progress report or report card. After the session, advisers contact the parents of students with unsatisfactory academic performance, excessive absenteeism, or unsatisfactory classroom conduct. We recommend a minimum of two advisement sessions per grading period. The information that follows provides the "nuts and bolts" of a schoolwide advisement program.

Goals

The primary goals of a schoolwide advisement program are to involve parents in their son's or daughter's education plan; to ensure each student's plan is appropriate and sufficient for a postsecondary education experience or entry into the modern workforce; to help students set realistic career and academic goals; and to implement a support system that provides time for frequent one-on-one contact with all students.

Objectives

- To establish and maintain rapport with students and parents.
- To establish a support system for students and parents.
- To promote communication between home and school by informing parents of their son's or daughter's progress toward completing an education plan.
- To monitor the academic progress of all students frequently.
- To provide early interventions for students who demonstrate deficits in one or more academic areas.
- To monitor the attendance and classroom conduct of students and provide early intervention for students who have chronic absenteeism and unsatisfactory conduct.
- To provide students with information on topics related to academics, colleges, careers, work ethics, drugs and alcohol, safety issues, and other areas deemed appropriate or necessary.
- To provide an opportunity for students and their parents to participate in an individual registration session with an adviser.
- To ensure students maximize their educational opportunities at each level.
- To ensure students have a solid education or career plan upon graduation from high school.

Organizational Steps

1. The school counselor will form a schoolwide advisement committee composed of students, parents, teachers, and staff. The committee members must be representative of the school's stakeholders.

2. The members will nominate and elect a committee chairperson.

3. The committee will establish a protocol for student group composition and adviser selection.

4. The committee will determine the advisement dates and bell schedule.

5. The committee will create group rosters that include advisers' names and room assignments.

6. The committee will conduct an informal survey of students to choose an official title for the schoolwide advisement program and to identify students' needs by grade level.

7. The committee will formulate annual student objectives for each grade level based on survey results.

8. The committee will develop session checklists for each advisement session.

9. The committee will develop activities and select materials for each advisement session.

Session Format

Before Session

- Advisers must review advisee roster and room location.
- Advisers must review advisement session objectives and materials.

During Session

- Advisers must take attendance.
- Advisers will distribute advisement materials to students and conduct mini-lesson.
- Advisers will conduct individual student conferences and complete individual student checklist.

After Session

- Advisers must contact parents when necessary.
- Advisers must refer students who are experiencing major difficulties to the school counselor.
- Advisers must return folders to the counseling office by the date specified.

The following forms are found in this section:

Forms 2.1 through 2.6 A-E

Forms 2.6 F-K through 2.11 A-E

Reflections/Lesson Learned

- Obtain support from school principal and administrative staff
- Keep it simple
- Start small and expand gradually
- Revisit lessons each year and revise in order to reflect changes in curriculum, career trends, and student needs
- Use the committee
- Monitor advisers' record keeping
- Keep students with the same adviser

SECTION 2: AN INDIVIDUAL ADVISEMENT PROGRAM

The implementation of an individual advisement program is the school counselor's primary responsibility. The program requires counselors to conduct individual thirty-minute conferences with all students and their parents annually. These conferences provide an opportunity for the counselor to individually review the student's current academic performance, to formulate or review long- and short-term educational goals, and to ensure course selections parallel education and career plans. The individual advisement session is an excellent opportunity for the school counselor to observe and document how a student is progressing in the academic, career, personal, and social domains. The program is ideal for building rapport and addressing parent and student questions or concerns.

Goals

The primary goals of the individual advisement program are to promote the career and educational development of all students and to ensure students have the necessary knowledge and skills to successfully transition to their postsecondary endeavors.

Objectives

- To develop rapport among the school counselors, students, and parents.
- To develop and solidify an individual education plan for each student.
- To ensure each student's career interests and goals parallel his or her six-year education plan.
- To review and discuss each student's academic performance regularly.
- To assess students' academic, career, and personal/social development.
- To ensure students are meeting necessary deadlines for completing college applications, SAT/ACT registrations, personal résumés, and job applications.

Organizational Steps

1. The individual advisement program is the primary responsibility of the school counselor.

2. A school's counseling staff must meet prior to the beginning of the new school year and review the school's counseling plan.

3. School counselors will review the counseling program's action plans for each grade level, which are based on the evaluation results from the previous year.

4. School counselors will develop individual advisement program session checklists that parallel the counseling program's goals and objectives.

5. School counselors will obtain a roster of all students assigned to their caseloads.

6. School counselors will schedule a thirty-minute appointment with each student and his or her parents for program planning and monitoring of academic progress.

7. School counselors will complete a checklist during each individual advisement session and give a copy to the student or his or her parents at the conclusion of the session.

8. School counselors must keep all completed checklists in a three-ring binder for future reference.

Session Format

Before Session

- The school counselor will distribute individual appointment slips to students at least three weeks in advance.
- The school counselor will review the advisement session checklist.
- The school counselor will review students' official school records (transcript, report card, and progress report).
- The school counselor will use the student's official school records to complete a Unit of Credit Checklist (high school students only).

During Session

- The school counselor will use the Individual Advisement Session Checklist as an agenda for the session.
- The school counselor will review the following information with the student and his or her parents:
  a. Current academic progress
  b. Unit of Credit Checklist (high school students only)
  c. Program of Study Commitment (high school students only)
  d. Individual Six-Year Education Plan (high school students only)
  e. Career portfolio
- The school counselor will address all questions or concerns of parents and student. The school counselor will copy the following documents and give them to parents or student at the conclusion of the meeting:
  a. Individual Advisement Session Checklist
  b. Unit of Credit Checklist (high school students only)
  c. Unofficial copy of the student's transcript
  d. Program of Study Commitment (high school students only)
  e. Individual Six-Year Education Plan (high school students only)

After Session

- The school counselor will contact parents to discuss student's information if they were unable to attend the meeting.
- The school counselor will follow up on items of concern.
- The school counselor will place completed documents in a three-ring binder.

The following forms are found in this section:

Forms 2.12A–C through 2.17

Reflection/Lessons Learned

- Keep it simple!
- Revisit the session checklist each year and revise in order to reflect changes in student needs.
- Follow up with parents who do not attend the individual session with their son or daughter.
- Follow up immediately with students who require more time than was allotted in their regular scheduled appointment.

SECTION 3: A RISING NINTH-GRADE ADVISEMENT PROGRAM

A rising ninth-grade advisement program is conducted annually with members of the school's administration, teachers, and counselors enthusiastically volunteering to serve as advisers. Advisers meet with eighth-grade students and their parents for an individual thirty-minute conference in order to orient new students to the high school, to explain graduation requirements, to design a six-year plan, and to establish rapport with students and parents. A school tour is an appealing attraction for new students and their parents during the advisement period. We suggest conducting day and evening advisement sessions during the semester preceding the students' entrance into ninth grade. We have found this program to be well received by middle school parents and the school community, and we have documented an increase in parent participation from 57% to 83% over the last two years. During the rising ninth-grade advisement program, advisers work hard to alleviate parent and student concerns about the high school experience and set the stage for future parent involvement.

Goals

The primary goals of the rising ninth-grade advisement program are to lay the foundation on which to build solid partnerships with students and parents; to inform students and parents of high school expectations and requirements; and to convey the importance of developing a comprehensive education and career plan based on the student's academic performance, personal needs, and career interests.

Objectives

- To conference individually with the rising ninth-grade students and their parents.
- To inform students and parents of the academic and nonacademic programs available at the high school.
- To inform students and parents of all graduation requirements.
- To inform parents and students of postsecondary options.

- To assist students with the registration process.
- To assist students with six-year program planning.
- To provide an opportunity for students and parents to meet faculty members and tour the high school.

Organizational Steps

1. The school advisement committee must meet prior to the start of the school year and develop program goals and objectives.

2. The committee must develop an advisement schedule (dates, times, and location) and request approval from both the middle and high schools' administration.

3. The committee must request a student roster from the feeder middle schools of rising ninth-grade students.

4. The committee must recruit high school faculty members to serve as advisers for the rising ninth-grade students.

5. The committee must assign students to advisers and type a master advisement roster.

6. The committee must send parent information and appointment request letters to the middle school to be distributed through eighth-grade homerooms.

7. A designated advisement committee member must obtain completed appointment slips from the middle school homeroom teachers or school counselor.

8. The advisement committee must review all appointment requests and construct a rising ninth-grade adviser master appointment schedule.

9. The advisement committee members will call rising ninth-grade parents and confirm all advisement appointments.

10. The advisement committee must distribute appointment schedules to all advisers one week prior to advisement dates.

11. All advisers will be provided with the directory information for all assigned advisees.

12. Advisers must contact each advisee the day immediately preceding the advisement appointment as a reminder to the parents of the advisement date, time, and location.

13. The advisement committee will conduct a training session for all advisers one week prior to the advisement dates.

14. All advisers will receive Individual Advisement Session Checklists prior to the advisement dates, to be completed during each advisement session.

15. The advisement sessions will be thirty minutes in length and parents will be given the opportunity to complete an evaluation form at the conclusion of the session.

Session Format

Before Session

- The adviser will review all student names on his or her advisement conference schedule.
- The adviser will call each student on the day preceding his or her appointment as a reminder of the scheduled conference time and location.
- The adviser will review each student's official school records (report card, progress report, standardized test scores, and attendance record) and registration form.
- The adviser will check for conference schedule changes (additions or deletions) prior to each advisement session.

During Session

- The adviser will use the Rising Ninth-Grade Advisement Program Conference Agenda with each student and discuss the information below:
  a. Explain objectives of conference
  b. Discuss the current school profile
  c. Review graduation requirements

    (1) Explain different paths and diploma choices.

    (2) Review total number of credits required for each program of study.

    (3) Explain and define core courses.

    (4) Review core course requirements for each diploma program.

    (5) Discuss sequence of core courses.

    (6) Discuss state graduation test and end of course tests.

  d. Review and discuss the student's academic history (last report card grades and attendance).
  e. Review and discuss four- to six-year program planning:

    (1) Discuss selecting a program of study.

    (2) Review the areas of concentration offered at the high school.

    (3) Review high school opportunity programs (job shadowing, apprenticeships, and dual enrollment).

    (4) Review postsecondary options (four-year college, technical college, special or proprietary schools, and armed services).

Note: Student's program of study selection should lead into his or her next two years of postsecondary education.

    f. Review and complete student's registration form.

    g. Discuss school's advisement system.

        (1) Schoolwide advisement program

        (2) Individual advisement program

    h. Address parent and student concerns and answer questions.

After Session

- Return the following items to the student's advisement folder:
  a. Agenda checklist
  b. Student registration form
  c. All copies of student's school records (report card, progress report, standardized test scores, and attendance record)

The following forms are found in this section:

Forms 2.18A through 2.22

Reflections/Lessons Learned

- Keep it simple!
- Reward faculty members for their hard work!
- Meet with the middle school faculty and staff in the fall to develop a timeline for all activities related to the rising ninth-grade advisement program.

FORM 2.1

Advisement Session Checklist

Grade: _____

SESSION NUMBER: _____   DATE: _____

BEFORE SESSION:

_____ (1) Review advisee roster and room location

_____ (2) Review all advisement session materials before the advisement session:

Lesson objectives: 1. _____

2. _____

3. _____

4. _____

Student reports: Report Card or Progress Report (**Circle**)

DURING SESSION:

_____ (1) Take attendance (see Form 2.3).

_____ (2) Conduct the advisement lesson with advisement group.

_____ (3) Instruct advisement group to study quietly while you conference with each student individually. Students may work on homework or read independently during who time period. **Students may not leave the advisement session!**

_____ (4) Discuss report cards or progress reports with each student. Advisers must praise students for all positive efforts and review appropriate study techniques for students who have not been successful during the grading period.

AFTER SESSION:

_____ (1) Send letters to parents of students who have failed courses during the reporting period. Document date on students' individual Advisement Objective Checklist (see Forms 2.6 A, B, C, D, or E).

_____ (2) Advisers must complete each student's Advisement Objectives Checklist after the advisement session. Record the date and note on this form all actions or suggestions given to the student.

_____ (3) Please return your ADVISER FOLDER to the Counseling Office by _____ (DATE).

FORM 2.2

Advisee Roster

School Year: _____

Adviser's Name: _____   Grade Level: _____

Adviser's Room Number: _____

	STUDENT NAME	ID NUMBER
1		
2		
3		
4		
5		
6		
7		
8		
9		
10		
11		
12		
13		
14		
15		

FORM 2.3

Advisee Attendance Record

School Year: _____

Directions: Please check attendance at the beginning of each advisement session and record a "P" (Present) or "A" (Absent) beside each student's name.

STUDENT NAME	Session __ Date:	Session __ Date:	Session __ Date:	Session __ Date:	Session __ Date:	Session __ Date:

FORM 2.4

Advisement Meeting Calendar

School Year: _____

SESSION 1	**PROGRESS REPORT**	DATE:
SESSION 2	**REPORT CARD**	DATE:
SESSION 3	**PROGRESS REPORT**	DATE:
SESSION 4	**REPORT CARD**	DATE:
SESSION 5	**REGISTRATION**	DATE:
SESSION 6	**REGISTRATION**	DATE:
SESSION 7	**PROGRESS REPORT**	DATE:
SESSION 8	**REPORT CARD**	DATE:
SESSION 9	**PROGRESS REPORT**	DATE:
SESSION 10	**REPORT CARD**	DATE:

FORM 2.5

Advisement Bell Schedule

School Year: _____

PERIODS	*TIME*
HOMEROOM	
FIRST PERIOD	
SECOND PERIOD	
ADVISEMENT PERIOD	
THIRD PERIOD	
FOURTH PERIOD	
LUNCH	
FIFTH PERIOD	
SIXTH PERIOD	

FORM 2.6A

Advisement Program Activities and Objectives Checklist

Student Name: _____   **School Year:** _____

Directions: Please complete the date and comments/actions sections of this form at the conclusion of the advisement session.

DATE	ADVISEMENT ACTIVITIES	COMMENTS/ACTIONS

FORM 2.6B

Sample Ninth-Grade Advisement Activities and Objectives Checklist

Student Name: _____   **School Year:** _____

Directions: Please complete the date and comments/actions sections of this form at the conclusion of the advisement session.

DATE	ADVISEMENT ACTIVITIES	COMMENTS/ ACTIONS

	Progress Report I Review
	  – Conference with student
	  – Contact parents/guardians (Failing 2 Classes, etc.)
	
	Lesson Objectives:
	  1. Orient Student to Support Services
	  2. Orient Student to Clubs
	  3. Review Study Skills and Time Management Information
	  4. Instruct Students to Complete the Student Information Form and Guidance Survey	

	Report Card I Review
	  – Conference with student
	  – Contact parents/guardians (Failing 2 Classes, etc.)
	
	Lesson Objectives:
	  1. Grades, Credits, Ranking, Semester Exams, and Grade Point Average
	  2. Review Student Transcript (GPA and RANK ONLY)	

	Progress Report II Review
	  – Conference with student
	  – Contact parents/guardians (Failing 2 Classes, etc.)
	
	Lesson Objective:
	  1. Eligibility and Graduation Requirements	

	Report Card II Review
	  – Conference with student
	  – Contact parents/guardians (Failing 2 Classes, etc.)
	
	Lesson Objectives:
	  1. Discuss Career Outlook and Work Ethic Information
	  2. Discuss Current Transcript (Class Rank and GPA)	

FORM 2.6B

Sample Ninth-Grade Advisement Activities
and Objectives Checklist (Continued)

DATE	ADVISEMENT ACTIVITIES	COMMENTS/ ACTIONS

	Registration for the next school year
	  – Review and select program of study
	  – Review graduation requirements
	  – Review student's transcript
	  – Select courses for the next school year	

	Progress Report III Review
	  – Conference with student
	  – Contact parents/guardians (Failing 2 Classes, etc.)
	
	Lesson Objectives:
	  1. Hope Scholarship and Hope Grant	

	Report Card III Review
	  – Conference with student
	  – Contact parents/guardians (Failing 2 Classes, etc.)
	
	Lesson Objectives:
	  1. Student Awards Information
	  2. Promotion Requirements
	  3. Summer School Information	

	Progress Report IV Review
	  – Conference with student
	  – Contact parents/guardians (Failing 2 Classes, etc.)
	
	Lesson Objective: Apprenticeship Program and PSAT
	  **Complete Advisement Program Evaluation	

FORM 2.6C

Sample Tenth-Grade Advisement Activities and Objectives Checklist

Student Name: _____   School Year: _____

Directions: Please complete the date and comments/actions sections of this form at the conclusion of the advisement session.

DATE	ADVISEMENT ACTIVITIES	COMMENTS/ ACTIONS

	Progress Report I Review
	   – Conference with student
	   – Contact parents/guardians (Failing 2 Classes, etc.)
	
	Lesson Objectives: PSAT
	   1. Orient Student to Support Services and Clubs
	   2. Discuss PSAT Information
	   3. Complete Student Information Form
	   4. Complete Advisement Survey	

	Report Card I Review
	   – Conference with student
	   – Contact parents/guardians (Failing 2 Classes, etc.)
	
	Lesson Objectives:
	   1. Review Qualifications for Driving Permits and License
	   2. Review Class Rank and Grade Point Average Information	

	Progress Report II Review
	   – Conference with student
	   – Contact parents/guardians (Failing 2 Classes, etc.)
	
	Lesson Objectives:
	   1. Preparing for Final Exams
	   2. Discuss Career Outlook and Work Ethic Information	

	Report Card II Review
	   – Conference with student
	   – Contact parents/guardians (Failing 2 Classes, etc.)
	
	Lesson Objectives:
	   1. Review Program of Study
	   2. Review Graduation Requirements
	   3. Review Promotion Requirements	

FORM 2.6C

Sample Tenth-Grade Advisement Activities and Objectives Checklist (Continued)

DATE	ADVISEMENT ACTIVITIES	COMMENTS/ ACTIONS
	Registration for the next school year – Review and select program of study – Review graduation requirements and AP courses – Review student's transcript – Select courses for the next school year	
	Progress Report III Review – Conference with student – Contact parents/guardians (Failing 2 Classes, etc.) Lesson Objectives: 1. Discuss Hope Scholarship, Hope Grant, and PSO Program Information	
	Report Card III Review – Conference with student – Contact parents/guardians (Failing 2 Classes, etc.) Lesson Objectives: 1. Provide and Discuss Summer School and Evening School Information 2. Discuss Student Awards: Honor Student, etc.	
	Progress Report IV Review – Conference with student – Contact parents/guardians (Failing 2 Classes, etc.) Lesson Objectives: 1. Discuss Youth Apprenticeship Program 2. Discuss SAT, ACT, and ASSET Information **Complete Advisement Program Evaluation	

FORM 2.6D

Sample Eleventh-Grade Advisement Activities and Objectives Checklist

Student Name: _____   School Year: _____

Directions: Please complete the date and comments/actions sections of this form at the conclusion of the advisement session.

DATE	ADVISEMENT ACTIVITIES	COMMENTS/ ACTIONS
	Progress Report I Review – Conference with student – Contact parents/guardians (Failing 2 Classes, etc.) Lesson Objectives: PSAT 1. Orient Student to Support Services and Clubs 2. Discuss GHSGT, SAT, and ACT 3. Complete Student Information Form 4. Complete Advisement Survey Form	
	Report Card I Review – Conference with student – Contact parents/guardians (Failing 2 Classes, etc.) Lesson Objectives: 1. Discuss College Visit Information 2. Discuss College Application Process	
	Progress Report II Review – Conference with student – Contact parents/guardians (Failing 2 Classes, etc.) Lesson Objectives: 1. Discuss Best Practices for Preparing for Final Exams 2. Discuss Career Outlook and Work Ethic Information	
	Report Card II Review – Conference with student – Contact parents/guardians (Failing 2 Classes, etc.) Lesson Objectives: 1. Review Graduation Requirements 2. Review Promotion Requirements 3. Review Class Ranking and Grade Point Average	

FORM 2.6D

Sample Eleventh-Grade Advisement
Activities and Objectives Checklist (Continued)

DATE	ADVISEMENT ACTIVITIES	COMMENTS/ ACTIONS
	Registration for the next school year – Review and select program of study – Review graduation, PSO requirements, and AP courses – Review student's transcript – Select courses for the next school year	
	Progress Report III Review – Conference with student – Contact parents/guardians (Failing 2 Classes, etc.) Lesson Objectives: 1. Discuss Financial Aid Information 2. Discuss PSO Information	
	Report Card III Review – Conference with student – Contact parents/guardians (Failing 2 Classes, etc.) Lesson Objectives: 1. Discuss Summer School and Evening School Information 2. Discuss GHSGT HELP Class Information	
	Progress Report IV Review – Conference with student – Contact parents/guardians (Failing 2 Classes, etc.) Lesson Objectives: 1. Discuss Youth Apprenticeship Program **Complete Advisement Program Evaluation	

FORM 2.6E

Sample Twelfth-Grade Advisement Activities and Objectives Checklist

Student Name: _____   **School Year**: _____

Directions: Please complete the date and comments/actions sections of this form at the conclusion of the advisement session.

DATE	ADVISEMENT ACTIVITIES	COMMENTS/ ACTIONS

	Progress Report I Review
	  – Conference with student
	  – Contact parents/guardians (Failing Any Classes, etc.)
	
	Lesson Objectives:
	  1. Review Senior Project Requirements and Senior Supplies
	  2. Orient Student to SAT, ACT, and ASSET
	  3. Encourage students to take SAT or ACT ASAP
	  4. Discuss FAST WEB and SCHOLARSHIP SEARCH
	  5. Discuss Armed Services and College Visits	

	Report Card I Review
	  – Conference with student
	  – Contact parents/guardians (Failing Any Classes, etc.)
	
	Lesson Objectives:
	  1. Create Time Line for College/Career Decisions
	  2. Discuss College Application Process
	  3. Discuss HOPE Scholarship and HOPE Grant Information	

	Progress Report II Review
	  – Conference with student
	  – Contact parents/guardians (Failing Any Classes, etc.)
	
	Lesson Objectives:
	  1. Discuss Creating a Great Résumé
	  2. Discuss Career Outlook and Work Ethic Information	

	Report Card II Review
	  – Conference with student
	  – Contact parents/guardians (Failing Any Classes, etc.)	

FORM 2.6E

Sample Twelfth-Grade Advisement
Activities and Objectives Checklist (Continued)

DATE	ADVISEMENT ACTIVITIES	COMMENTS/ ACTIONS
	Lesson Objectives: 1. Review Graduation Requirements 2. Review Night School Information 3. Review Class Rank and Grade Point Average Information	
	Progress Report III Review – Conference with student – Contact parents/guardians (Failing Any Classes, etc.) Lesson Objective: 1. Applying for HOPE and Financial Aid Information	
	Report Card III Review – Conference with student – Contact parents/guardians (Failing Any Classes, etc.) Lesson Objective: 1. Review Time Line from Session 3	
	Progress Report IV Review – Conference with student – Contact parents/guardians (Failing Any Classes, etc.) Lesson Objective: 1. Senior Seminar (Share Decisions) *Advisement Program Evaluation	

FORM 2.6F

Sample Middle Grades Advisement Activities and Objectives Checklist

Student Name: _____   School Year: _____

Directions: Please complete the date and comments/actions sections of this form at the conclusion of the advisement session.

DATE	ADVISEMENT ACTIVITIES	COMMENTS/ ACTIONS

	Progress Report I Review
	  − Conference with student
	  − Contact parents/guardians (Failing Any Classes, etc.)
	
	Lesson Objectives:
	  1. Orientation to schoolwide advisement program
	  2. Orientation to school counseling services
	  3. Orientation to school clubs and organizations	

	Report Card I Review
	  − Conference with student
	  − Contact parents/guardians (Failing Any Classes, etc.)
	
	Lesson Objectives:
	  1. Study Skills
	  2. School Tutoring Programs and/or Services	

	Progress Report II Review
	  − Conference with student
	  − Contact parents/guardians (Failing Any Classes, etc.)
	
	Lesson Objectives:
	  1. Organization and Outlining Skills
	  2. Promotion Requirements	

	Report Card II Review
	  − Conference with student
	  − Contact parents/guardians (Failing Any Classes, etc.)
	
	Lesson Objectives:
	  1. Test-taking Strategies
	  2. Decision-making Skills	

FORM 2.6F

Sample Middle Grades Advisement
Activities and Objectives Checklist (Continued)

DATE	ADVISEMENT ACTIVITIES	COMMENTS/ ACTIONS
	Progress Report III Review – Conference with student – Contact parents/guardians (Failing Any Classes, etc.) Lesson Objective: 1. Career Interest Inventories 2. Exploration of Career Paths	
	Report Card III Review – Conference with student – Contact parents/guardians (Failing Any Classes, etc.) Lesson Objective: 1. Note-taking Skills 2. Discuss Dangers and/or Pressures That May Confront Students	
	Progress Report IV Review – Conference with student – Contact parents/guardians (Failing Any Classes, etc.) Lesson Objective: 1. Discuss Factual Information About the Use and Abuse of Drugs, Alcohol, and Tobacco Products 2. Review Appropriate Safety Strategies 3. Review Appropriate Support People and/or Services That Could Be Helpful to Students *Advisement Program Evaluation	

FORM 2.6G
Sample Ninth-Grade Schoolwide
Advisement Program Activities/Topics

AREA	*ACTIVITIES/TOPICS*
GENERAL	<ul><li>Orientation to schoolwide advisement program</li><li>Orientation to school counseling services</li><li>Eligibility for participation in extracurricular activities</li><li>Summer and night school program opportunities</li><li>Tutoring programs or services</li><li>Academic student awards for ninth grade</li></ul>
ACADEMIC	<ul><li>Study skills</li><li>Time management</li><li>Learning styles</li><li>Educational goal setting</li><li>Identify personal strengths and weaknesses in academic areas</li><li>Identify reason for postsecondary education</li><li>High School terms: credits, class rank, semester exam, grade point average, and transcript (Official and Unofficial)</li><li>Promotion requirements</li><li>Graduation requirements</li><li>Preparing for final exams</li><li>PSAT information and tips for test preparation</li><li>Specific scholarship and grant information (Example: Georgia HOPE Scholarship Program)</li><li>High school programs of study</li><li>Registration for the next school year</li></ul>
CAREER	<ul><li>Steps of decision making</li><li>Work ethic: Responsibility</li><li>Time management and task management skills</li><li>Identify and appreciate personal interests, abilities, and skills</li><li>How individual characteristics relate to achieving personal, social, educational, and career goals</li><li>Interpersonal skills required for working with and for others</li><li>How to locate and evaluate information about career possibilities</li><li>Use relevant resources to plan and make decisions about training and future education needs (e.g., Internet, Occupational Outlook Handbook)</li><li>Develop an individual career plan and start a career planning portfolio</li><li>Select course work that is related to career interests</li></ul>
PERSONAL/ SOCIAL	<ul><li>The importance of identifying personal strengths, weaknesses, assets, attitudes, values, and beliefs</li><li>The goal setting process</li><li>The importance of recognizing and accepting individual differences</li><li>The importance of respecting and recognizing alternative points of view</li><li>Appropriate ways of communicating with others</li><li>Appropriate ways of dealing with peer pressure</li></ul>

FORM 2.6H

Sample Tenth-Grade Schoolwide
Advisement Program Activities/Topics

AREA	ACTIVITIES/TOPICS
GENERAL	➤ Orientation to schoolwide advisement program ➤ Orientation to school counseling services ➤ Eligibility for participation in extracurricular activities ➤ Qualifications for state driving permits and license ➤ Summer and night school programs ➤ Tutoring programs or services ➤ Academic student awards for tenth grade
ACADEMIC	➤ Study skills ➤ Set challenging educational goals ➤ Steps to become a self-directed and independent learner ➤ Reasons for a postsecondary education ➤ High School terms: credits, class rank, semester exam, grade point average, and transcript (Official and Unofficial) ➤ Promotion requirements ➤ Graduation requirements ➤ Preparing for final exams ➤ PSAT, SAT, ACT, and ASSET information and tips for test preparation ➤ Advanced Placement program and course information ➤ Registration for the next school year
CAREER	➤ Skills to make good decisions ➤ Work ethic: Dependability ➤ Pursue and develop competencies in areas of interest ➤ How to apply academic and vocational skills to personal interests ➤ The relationship between educational achievement and career planning ➤ Identify appropriate choices during high school that will lead to marketable skills for entry-level employment or advanced training ➤ Transferable skills that can apply to a variety of occupations and changing occupational requirements ➤ Skills necessary to compare education and job opportunities ➤ Academic and employment readiness skills utilized in work-based learning situations such as a job shadowing experience ➤ Review individual career plan and update career portfolio ➤ Select courses that are appropriated for tentative occupational interest
PERSONAL/ SOCIAL	➤ Assist students in identifying short- and long-term personal goals ➤ Assist students in developing an action plan to set and achieve realistic goals; explore alternative ways of achieving goals ➤ Discuss dangers and/or pressures that may confront student ➤ Review appropriate safety strategies ➤ Review appropriate support people and/or services that could be helpful to students ➤ Discuss factual information about the use and abuse of drugs, alcohol, and tobacco

FORM 2.6I
Sample Eleventh-Grade Schoolwide Advisement Program Activities/Topics

AREA	ACTIVITIES/TOPICS
GENERAL	➤ Review of school counseling services ➤ Develop timeline of important events (e.g., creating a résumé, taking the SAT or ACT, visiting colleges) ➤ Summer and night school programs ➤ Tutoring programs or services ➤ Academic student awards for eleventh grade
ACADEMIC	➤ Graduation requirements ➤ Promotion requirements ➤ PSAT, SAT, ACT, and ASSET test dates, registration, and tips for test preparation ➤ PSAT and the National Merit Scholarship program ➤ How to utilize individual assessment results in education planning ➤ Tips and resources for conducting a college search ➤ Tips for arranging a college visit ➤ Financial aid for postsecondary education ➤ Advanced Placement program and course information ➤ Registration for the next school year
CAREER	➤ Work ethic: Punctuality and Integrity ➤ Discuss the career planning process ➤ How to evaluate and interpret career information ➤ The relationship between educational achievement and career planning ➤ How to use a range of resources (e.g., handbooks, career materials, labor market information, and computerized career information delivery systems) ➤ Advantages and disadvantages of self-employment as a career option ➤ Locate, interpret, and use information about job openings and opportunities ➤ How to make tentative educational and occupational choices ➤ Review or discuss postsecondary technical and academic programs ➤ Academic and employment readiness skills in work-based learning situations such as internship experiences ➤ Review individual career plan and update career portfolio ➤ Select courses that are appropriated for tentative occupational interest
PERSONAL/ SOCIAL	➤ Review the value of persistence and perseverance in acquiring knowledge and skills ➤ Review effective problem-solving and decision-making strategies to make safe and healthy choices ➤ Discuss dangers and/or pressures that may confront student ➤ Discuss factual information about the use and abuse of drugs, alcohol, and tobacco

FORM 2.6J
Sample Twelfth-Grade Schoolwide
Advisement Program Activities/Topics

AREA	ACTIVITIES/TOPICS
GENERAL	➢ Review of school counseling services ➢ Develop timeline of important events (e.g., creating a résumé, taking the SAT or ACT, visiting colleges) ➢ Summer and night school programs ➢ Armed Service Registration for male students ➢ Voter Registration ➢ Tutoring programs or services ➢ Academic student awards for twelfth grade
ACADEMIC	➢ Review graduation requirements ➢ Advanced Placement program and course information ➢ Tips for arranging a college visit ➢ Identify and pair postsecondary options with interests, achievements, aptitude, and abilities ➢ PSAT, SAT, ACT, and ASSET test dates, registration, and tips for test preparation ➢ Create a college and/or career decisions timeline ➢ Tips on completing college applications ➢ Discuss the financial aid process
CAREER	➢ Work ethic: Initiative and Effort ➢ Discuss the concepts of career ladders ➢ Discuss the advantages and disadvantages of nontraditional occupations ➢ Review how to utilize school and community resources to explore education and occupation choices ➢ Acquire the knowledge that there could be changes that may require retraining and upgrading of employment skills ➢ Career plans reflect the importance of lifelong learning ➢ How to make tentative educational and occupational choices ➢ Review or discuss postsecondary technical and academic programs ➢ Academic and employment readiness skills used in work-based learning situations such as mentoring and/or a graduation project ➢ Review the skills and behaviors necessary for a successful job interview ➢ Discuss the skills necessary for preparing a résumé and completing job applications ➢ Review individual career plan and update career portfolio
PERSONAL/ SOCIAL	➢ Review information pertaining to emotional and physical dangers of substance use and abuse ➢ Coping skills necessary for managing life events

FORM 2.6K

Sample Middle Grades Schoolwide Advisement Program Activities/Topics

AREA	ACTIVITIES/TOPICS
GENERAL	➢ Orientation to schoolwide advisement program ➢ Orientation to counseling services ➢ Orientation to school clubs and organizations ➢ Eligibility for participation in extracurricular activities ➢ Tutoring programs or services ➢ Academic student awards for grades 6, 7, and 8
ACADEMIC	➢ Study skills ➢ Note-taking skills ➢ Organizational and outlining skills ➢ Listening skills ➢ Test-taking strategies ➢ Promotion requirements ➢ Registration for the next school year
CAREER	➢ Decision-making skills ➢ Problem-solving skills ➢ Work ethics and positive character traits ➢ Career interest inventories ➢ Exploration of career paths ➢ Identify short- and long-term goals
PERSONAL/SOCIAL	➢ Conflict resolution ➢ Discuss dangers and/or pressures that may confront students ➢ Review appropriate safety strategies ➢ Review appropriate support people and/or services that could be helpful to students ➢ Discuss factual information about the use and abuse of drugs, alcohol, and tobacco

FORM 2.7

Individual Student Data

NAME: _____

       LAST   FIRST   MIDDLE

ADDRESS: _____

_____

_____

       STREET   CITY   STATE   ZIP

HOME TELEPHONE: _____

DATE OF BIRTH: _____   AGE: _____   GENDER: _____

MOTHER: _____

       LAST   FIRST   MIDDLE

ADDRESS: _____

       STREET   CITY   STATE   ZIP

HOME TELEPHONE: _____   WORK TELEPHONE: _____

CELLULAR TELEPHONE: _____   E-MAIL ADDRESS: _____

MOTHER'S EMPLOYMENT: _____

FATHER: _____

       LAST   FIRST   MIDDLE

ADDRESS: _____

       STREET   CITY   STATE   ZIP

HOME TELEPHONE: _____   WORK TELEPHONE: _____

CELLULAR TELEPHONE: _____   E-MAIL ADDRESS: _____

FATHER'S EMPLOYMENT: _____

STUDENT'S CURRENT HIGH SCHOOL PROGRAM:
(Circle One) College Prep Career/Tech Other

STUDENT'S ACADEMIC INTEREST: _____

STUDENT'S CAREER INTEREST : _____

STUDENT'S QUESTIONS OR CONCERNS: _____

_____

_____

_____

FORM 2.8

School Counselor Referral

Date: _____

Referring Teacher or Adviser: _____ Course: _____

Student Name: _____ Grade: _____

Nature of Referral:

_____ Academic _____ Attendance _____ Discipline

_____ Other: _____

Problem as seen by referring teacher or adviser:

_____

_____

_____

_____

_____

_____

Attempts made by teacher or adviser to alleviate the problem:

_____ Conference with Student
_____ Conference with Parent
_____ Contacted Parent (Telephone, Letter, or E-Mail)

School Counselor's Response:

_____

_____

_____

_____

_____

_____

FORM 2.9

Letter of Concern

**(We suggest using the school's
official stationery for this letter to parents)**

Date _____

Dear _____ (Parent's Name):

_____ (Student's Name) _____ report card or progress report was sent home on

_____ (Date of report) _____ . I am concerned about his or her grades, attendance, and/or conduct in the following subject areas:

SUBJECT	GRADE	ABSENCES	CONDUCT	TEACHER

Please contact the school's counseling office to make an appointment to meet with your child's teachers and school counselor.

Sincerely,
[Adviser's Name]

FORM 2.10

Good News Gram

GOOD NEWS GRAM

FOR

_____

Student's Name

Improvements in:

☐ Attendance   ☐ Grades   ☐ Homework   ☐ Conduct

Comments:

School's Return Address   STAMP

_____

_____

_____

FORM 2.11A

Sample Schoolwide Advisement Program Evaluation

NINTH GRADE

School Year: _____

The following were topics presented or activities conducted during the advisement sessions this school year. Please check each topic that you found to be beneficial and/or informative.

_____ 1. Orientation to the school's Counseling Department (Services, Policies, etc.)

_____ 2. Orientation to clubs and how to join school organizations

_____ 3. Review of study skills and time management strategies

_____ 4. Review of high school terms: transcripts, credits, class rank, semester exams, and grade point average

_____ 5. Discussion on how to prepare for final exams

_____ 6. Review of eligibility criteria and graduation requirements

_____ 7. Discussion on career outlook

_____ 8. Discussion on work ethic

_____ 9. Participation in registration activities

_____ 10. Orientation to scholarship and grant information

_____ 11. Review of student awards, promotion requirements, and summer school information

_____ 12. Discussion on job shadowing and PSAT

_____ 13. Enjoyed refreshments brought by my adviser

_____ 14. Enjoyed the *Good News Grams* that I received from my adviser

_____ 15. I feel that the advisement program provides me with beneficial information and assists me with educational and career planning

Please list topics that you feel would benefit <u>all 9th grade</u> students:

_____

_____

_____

FORM 2.11B

Sample Schoolwide Advisement Program Evaluation

TENTH GRADE

School Year: _____

The following were topics presented or activities conducted during the advisement sessions this school year. Please check each topic that you found to be beneficial and/or informative.

_____ 1. Orientation to the school's Counseling Department (Services, Policies, etc.)

_____ 2. Orientation to clubs and how to join school organizations

_____ 3. Discussion of specific tests: PSAT, ACT, SAT, and ASSET

_____ 4. Review of qualifications for driving permits and license

_____ 5. Review of high school terms: transcript, class rank, and grade point average

_____ 6. Discussion on how to prepare for final exams

_____ 7. Discussion on how to find a job

_____ 8. Review of program of study, promotion, graduation, and eligibility requirements

_____ 9. Discussion of Advanced Placement courses

_____ 10. Discussion of Postsecondary Option Program

_____ 11. Orientation to scholarship and grant information

_____ 12. Review of student awards (Honor Student, etc.)

_____ 13. Discussion of Evening and Summer School Programs

_____ 14. Discussion of Youth Apprenticeship program

_____ 15. Enjoyed refreshments brought by my adviser

_____ 16. Enjoyed the *Good News Grams* that I received from my adviser

_____ 17. I feel that the advisement program provides me with beneficial information that assists me with educational and career planning

Please list topics that you feel would benefit <u>all 10th grade</u> students:

_____

_____

_____

FORM 2.11C

Sample Schoolwide Advisement Program Evaluation

ELEVENTH GRADE

School Year: _____

The following were topics presented or activities conducted during the advisement sessions this school year. Please check each topic that you found to be beneficial and/or informative.

_____ 1. Orientation to the school's Counseling Department (Services, Policies, etc.)

_____ 2. Discussion of the Georgia High School Graduation Tests, PSAT, ACT, SAT, and ASSET

_____ 3. Discussion on college visits and college application process

_____ 4. Discussion on how to prepare for final exams

_____ 5. Discussion on career outlook and work ethic information

_____ 6. Review of graduation and promotion requirements, class rank, and grade point average

_____ 7. Discussion of Advanced Placement courses

_____ 8. Discussion of Postsecondary Option Program

_____ 9. Discussion of financial aid information

_____ 10. Orientation to the Hope Scholarship and Hope Grant

_____ 11. Review of student awards and honors night

_____ 12. Discussion of Evening and Summer School Programs

_____ 13. Discussion of Youth Apprenticeship Program

_____ 14. Discussion of the senior timeline/calendar

_____ 15. Enjoyed refreshments brought by my adviser

_____ 16. Enjoyed the *Good News Grams* that I received from my adviser

_____ 17. I feel that the advisement program provides me with beneficial information that assists me with educational and career planning

Please list topics that you feel would benefit <u>all 11th grade</u> students:

_____

_____

_____

FORM 2.11D

Sample Schoolwide Advisement Program Evaluation

TWELFTH GRADE

School Year: _____

The following were topics presented or activities conducted during the advisement sessions this school year. Please check each topic that you found to be beneficial and/or informative.

_____ 1. Orientation to the school's Counseling Department (Services, Policies, etc.)

_____ 2. Review of graduation and promotion requirements, class rank, and grade point average

_____ 3. Discussion of specific tests: High School Graduation, PSAT, ACT, SAT, and ASSET

_____ 4. Discussion on college visits and college application process

_____ 5. Review of the financial aid process

_____ 6. Discussion on FAST WEB, scholarship search, and grant process

_____ 7. Discussion on how to find a job

_____ 8. Discussion on how to enlist in the Armed Services

_____ 9. Create a timeline for college/career decisions

_____ 10. Discussion on creating a great résumé

_____ 11. Discussion on job interview skills

_____ 12. Review of student awards (Valedictorian, Salutatorian, Honor Student, etc.)

_____ 13. Discussion of Evening and Summer School Programs

_____ 14. Enjoyed refreshments brought by my adviser

_____ 15. Enjoyed the *Good News Grams* that I received from my adviser

_____ 16. I feel that the advisement program provides me with beneficial information that assists me with educational and career planning

Please list topics that you feel would benefit <u>all 12th grade</u> students:

_____

_____

_____

FORM 2.11E

Sample Schoolwide Advisement Program Evaluation

MIDDLE GRADES

School Year: _____

The following were topics presented or activities conducted during the advisement sessions this school year. Please check each topic that you found to be beneficial and/or informative.

_____ 1. Orientation to the school's Counseling Department (Services, Policies, etc.)

_____ 2. Orientation to the school's clubs and organizations

_____ 3. Discussion on the eligibility requirements for participating in extracurricular activities

_____ 4. Review of tutoring programs and services

_____ 5. Review of good study skills

_____ 6. Review of note-taking skills

_____ 7. Review of organizational and outlining skills

_____ 8. Review of listening skills

_____ 9. Review of test-taking strategies

_____ 10. Discussion on promotion requirements

_____ 11. Discussion on decision-making and problem-solving skills

_____ 12. Review of student awards for each grade level

_____ 13. Information on how to deal with conflict

_____ 14. Enjoyed refreshments brought by my adviser

_____ 15. Enjoyed the *Good News Grams* that I received from my adviser

_____ 16. I feel that the advisement program provides me with beneficial information that assists me with educational and career planning

Please list topics that you feel would benefit (circle grade level) 6th, 7th, or 8th grade students:

_____

_____

_____

FORM 2.12A

Individual Advisement Session Checklist

9th and 10th Grades

Student Name: _____ Date: _____

_____ 1. Program of study: College Prep, Career Tech Prep, Dual Seal (CP and CT), or Special Education

_____ 2. Area of concentration: _____

_____ 3. Review total credits earned: _____

Total credits required for graduation: _____

_____ 4. Review current schedule (first and second semester)

_____ 5. Review current classroom performance problem areas:

_____

_____ 6. Review current GPA and class ranking

_____ 7. Review school organizations and/or extracurricular activities:

Student membership: _____

_____ 8. Review PSO and Youth Apprenticeship Programs: _____

_____ 9. Summer School or Evening School: recommended or student requested course/courses: _____

_____ 10. Discuss 4–6 Year Plan: Tech College   2-Year College
4-Year College   Work

_____ 11. Career goals/plans: _____

_____ 12. Review career portfolio: _____

_____ 13. Parent/Parents attended conference: Yes or No

Parent concerns: _____

_____ 14. Student must pass all sections of the State Graduation Test, which is administered in the _____ grade, and complete all requirements for a designated program of study in order to receive a Regular High School Diploma.

_____ 15. PSAT information

_____ 16. State scholarship information

_____ 17. Academic awards information

Additional information: _____

Student signature: _____

Parent signature: _____

Counselor signature: _____

FORM 2.12B

Individual Advisement Session Checklist

11th and 12 Grades

STUDENT NAME: _____ DATE: _____

_____ Program of study: College Prep, Career Tech Prep, Dual Seal (CP and CT), or Special Education

_____ Area of concentration: _____

_____ Review total credits earned: _____

_____ Review of total credits needed to fulfill all graduation requirements: _____

_____ Review of remaining courses needed for graduation:

Core courses: _____

Career Tech courses: _____

Electives: _____

_____ Review of current schedule

_____ Review High School Graduation Tests results:

Writing: PASS   OR   FAIL

Language Arts: PASS   OR   FAIL

Social Studies: PASS   OR   FAIL

Mathematics: PASS   OR   FAIL

Science: PASS   OR   FAIL

_____ Review of student's test results:

PSAT score: _____

ASVAB score: _____

SAT scores: _____

ASSET scores: _____

ACT scores: _____

FORM 2.12B

Individual Advisement Session Checklist (Continued)

_____ Review of course requests for the next school year (if applicable)

_____ Review of CUMULATIVE GPA _____ CLASS RANK _____

_____ Summer School or Night School: recommended or student requested course/ courses: _____

_____ Review state scholarship information and qualifications:

_____ Review of student's progress toward completing 4–6 year plan:

_____ Career interest: _____

_____ Completed a job application

_____ College interest: _____

_____ Completed a résumé

_____ Completed and sent college application

_____ Completed the FAFSA packet

_____ Completed scholarship and financial aid packets

_____ Parent/Parents or Guardian attended conference: Yes or No

Parent concerns: _____

_____

Additional information: _____

_____

Student signature: _____

Counselor signature: _____

Parent signature: _____

FORM 2.12C

Individual Advisement Session Checklist

Middle Grades

Student Name: _____ Date: _____

_____ 1. Review academic progress

_____ 2. Review schedule (first and second semester)

_____ 3. Review current classroom performance

Problem areas: _____

_____ 4. Summer School or Evening School: recommended or student requested
          course/courses: _____

_____ 5. Review study skills

_____ 6. Academic awards information

_____ 7. Review school organizations and/or extracurricular
          activities:

Student membership: _____

_____ 8. Career interests: _____

_____ 9. Introduce or review career portfolio: _____

_____ 10. Postsecondary interest:

          Tech College   2-Year College   4-Year College   Work

_____ 11. Review State Assessment information and results

_____ 12. Peer relations/friendship issues: _____

_____ 13. Parent/Parents attended conference: Yes or No

Parent concerns: _____

_____

Additional information:_____

_____

Student signature: _____

Parent signature: _____

FORM 2.13A

Unit of Credit Checklist

College Preparatory Program

Name: _____   Homeroom: _____

_____ Total Units Required for the College Preparatory Program of Study

NOTE: A=First Semester Course   B=Second Semester Course

English (_____Units Required)

☐ 9A   ☐ 10A   ☐ 11A   ☐ 12A   ☐ Other: _____

☐ 9B   ☐ 10B   ☐ 11B   ☐ 12B   ☐ Other: _____

- -

Math (_____Units Required)

☐ Algebra 1A   ☐ Geometry A   ☐ Algebra 2A   ☐ Other: _____

☐ Algebra 1B   ☐ Geometry B   ☐ Algebra 2B   ☐ Other: _____

☐ Adv Alg/Trig A   ☐ Algebra 3A   ☐ Calculus A

☐ Adv Alg/Trig B   ☐ Algebra 3B   ☐ Calculus B

- -

Science (_____Units Required)

☐ Intro Physics A   ☐ Biology A   ☐ Physics A   ☐ Chemistry A

☐ Intro Physics B   ☐ Biology B   ☐ Physics B   ☐ Chemistry B

☐ Anatomy A   ☐ Other: _____

☐ Anatomy B   ☐ Other: _____

- -

Social Studies (_____ Units Required)

☐ World History A   ☐ American History A   ☐ Citizenship/Civics

☐ World History B   ☐ American History B   ☐ Other _____

☐ Psychology   ☐ Sociology   ☐ World Geography   ☐ Economics

                                                             ☐ Other _____

- -

Physical Education (_____ Units Required)

☐ Health/Safety   ☐ Personal Fitness

- -

FORM 2.13A

Unit of Credit Checklist (Continued)

Foreign Language (_____Units Required)

☐ Spanish 1A   ☐ Spanish 2A   ☐ German 1A   ☐ French 1A

☐ Spanish 1B   ☐ Spanish 2B   ☐ German 1B   ☐ French 1B

☐ Other: _____

- -

Electives (_____ Units Required)

1. _____   3. _____   5. _____   7. _____

2. _____   4. _____   6. _____   8. _____

FORM 2.13B

Unit Career Technical Preparatory

Name: _____   Homeroom: _____

Area of Concentration: _____

_____ Total Units Required for the Technology/Career Preparatory Program of Study

NOTE: A=First Semester Course   B=Second Semester Course

English (_____Units Required)

☐ 9A	☐ 10A	☐11A	☐ 12A	☐ Other: _____
☐ 9B	☐ 10B	☐11B	☐ 12B	☐ Other: _____

- -

Math (_____Units Required)

☐ Appl Problem Solving A		☐ Applied Algebra A
☐ Appl Problem Solving B		☐ Applied Algebra B
☐ Appl Geometry A		☐ Other: _____
☐ Appl Geometry B		☐ Other: _____
☐ Applied Algebra II A	☐ CP Algebra 1A	☐ CP Geometry A
☐ Applied Algebra II B	☐ CP Algebra 1B	☐ CP Geometry B

- -

Science (_____Units Required)

☐ Applied Physics A	☐ Applied Biology A	☐ Applied Chemistry A
☐ Applied Physics B	☐ Applied Biology B	☐ Applied Chemistry B
☐ CP Intro Physics A	☐ CP Biology A	☐ Other: _____
☐ CP Intro Physics B	☐ CP Biology B	
☐ Other: _____		

- -

Social Studies (_____Units Required)

☐ World History A	☐ American History A	☐ Citizenship/Civics
☐ World History B	☐ American History B	☐ Economics
☐ World Geography	☐ Other _____	
	☐ Other _____	

FORM 2.13B

Unit Career Technical Preparatory (Continued)

Physical Education (_____ Units Required)

☐ Health/Safety   ☐ Personal Fitness

- -

Technology/Career Preparatory (_____ Units Required)

1. _____   3. _____   5. _____   7. _____

2. _____   4. _____   6. _____   8. _____

Electives (_____ Units Required)

1. _____   3. _____   5. _____   7. _____

2. _____   4. _____   6. _____   8. _____

FORM 2.14

Program of Study Commitment Grades 9–12

STUDENT NAME: _____   DATE: _____

Please review the programs of study offered at _____ High School and the total units required for graduation. Discuss the information with your parents and select the program you plan to pursue during the next four years. Students pursuing the Career Technical Preparatory Program of Study must select an area of concentration in a specific Career Technical area. Students and their parents must sign the form below indicating that they understand the graduation requirements for the program of study that they will pursue while attending _____ High School.

Programs of Study

_____ College Preparatory
_____ Technology/Career Preparatory

T/C Areas of Concentration

_____ Agriculture
_____ Automotive/Small Engines
_____ Business, Marketing, and Information Systems
_____ Construction
_____ Drafting
_____ Family & Consumer Science
_____ Graphic Arts
_____ Health Occupations
_____ JROTC
_____ Metal Working
_____ Technology

PROGRAM OF STUDY UNIT REQUIREMENTS

SUBJECT AREA	COLLEGE PREP	TECHNOLOGY/CAREER
English	_____ Total Units	_____ Total Units
Mathematics	_____ Total Units	_____ Total Units
Science	_____ Total Units	_____ Total Units
Social Studies	_____ Total Units	_____ Total Units
Physical Education	_____ Total Units	_____ Total Units
Foreign Language	_____ Total Units	_____ Total Units
Technology/Career	_____ Total Units	_____ Total Units
Local Electives	_____ Total Units	_____ Total Units

Student Signature: _____   Parent Signature: _____

FORM 2.15A

Individual Six-Year Education Plan

Required Units	9th Grade	10th Grade	11th Grade	12th Grade	1st Year Postsecondary	2nd Year Postsecondary
English CP = _____ CT = _____						
Math CP = _____ CT = _____						
Science CP = _____ CT = _____						
Social Studies CP = _____ CT = _____						
Foreign Language CP = _____ CT = _____						
Physical Education CP = _____ CT = _____						
Career Tech Courses CP = _____ CT = _____						
Elective Courses CP = _____ CT = _____						

Note: CP = College Preparatory Program of Study   CT = Career Technical Program of Study

FORM 2.15B

Sample Individual Six-Year Education Plan (College Preparatory Program of Study)

Required Units	9th Grade	10th Grade	11th Grade	12th Grade	1st Year Postsecondary	2nd Year Postsecondary
English CP = _____ CT = _____	CP English 9	CP English 10	CP or AP American Lit/Comp 11	CP or AP English Lit/Comp 12		
Math CP = _____ CT = _____	CP Algebra I or CP Geometry	CP Algebra II or CP Geometry	CP Algebra 2 or Adv Algebra & Trig	Adv Algebra & Trig or AP Calculus		
Science CP = _____ CT = _____	CP Physics or CP Biology	CP Biology or CP Chemistry I	CP Chemistry I or Physics I	CP Chemistry II or AP Science Course		
Social Studies CP = _____ CT = _____	Citizenship	Word History	US History	Economics		
Foreign Language CP = _____ CT = _____	Spanish I	Spanish II	Spanish III	Spanish IV		
Physical Education CP = _____ CT = _____	Personal Fitness	Heath				
Career Tech Courses CP = _____ CT = _____						
Elective Courses CP = _____ CT = _____						

FORM 2.16

Individual Advisement Appointment Notice

(Postcard Format)

****

INDIVIDUAL ADVISEMENT APPOINTMENT

Dear _____ (Student Name) _____

An individual advisement appointment has been scheduled for _____ (Date) _____ at _____ (Time) _____ with your school counselor, _____ (Counselor's Name) _____. During the session, you will have an opportunity to ask questions and share your concerns about your high school experience. _____ (Counselor's Name) _____ will discuss or review the information below during the meeting:

Graduation Requirements   Postsecondary Career Plan
Review Test Results   Program of Study
Student's Questions or Concerns   Six-Year Educational Plan
Academic Records   Career Portfolio

Parents are encouraged to attend the individual advisement session with their son or daughter. The appointment will last approximately 30 minutes.

_____ is looking forward to meeting with you and your parents.

****

School's Return Address   STAMP

_____

_____

_____

****

FORM 2.17

Individual Advisement Program Parent/Student Survey

The Counseling Staff needs your assistance in assessing our Individual Advisement Program. Please complete the survey below by circling the response that best depicts your experience during the individual advisement session. This survey looks at various components of our program, and the results will reveal the progress that has been made toward accomplishing the goals and objectives stated in our Counseling Plan. Please write any additional comments on the back of the survey. Please fold and place the completed form in the evaluation box. THANK YOU!

KEY:

5 strongly agree 4 agree 3 undecided 2 disagree 1 strongly disagree

1. The school counselor began the appointment on time. 5 4 3 2 1

2. The school counselor was friendly and professional. 5 4 3 2 1

3. The school counselor used language that was easy to understand. 5 4 3 2 1

4. The school counselor presented the information in an organized way. 5 4 3 2 1

5. The school counselor reviewed my son's or daughter's current academic progress. 5 4 3 2 1

6. The school counselor reviewed my son's or daughter's program of study. 5 4 3 2 1

7. The school counselor reviewed the units of credit that my son or daughter has obtained up to this point. 5 4 3 2 1

8. The school counselor reviewed my son's or daughter's six-year education plan and assisted with the selection of courses for the next school year. 5 4 3 2 1

9. The school counselor provided information on standardized tests and upcoming registration dates for the PSAT, SAT, ACT, ASSET, ASVAB, and/or AP. 5 4 3 2 1

10. The school counselor provided information about tutorial services and programs. 5 4 3 2 1

11. The school counselor provided information about summer or night school programs. 5 4 3 2 1

12. The school counselor discussed the college application process. 5 4 3 2 1

13. The school counselor discussed the financial aid process. 5 4 3 2 1

14. The school counselor discussed my son's or daughter's career interests and reviewed his or her career portfolio. 5 4 3 2 1

15. The individual advisement session was productive and helped me to better understand what my son or daughter is doing to prepare for postsecondary experiences. 5 4 3 2 1

FORM 2.18A

Rising Ninth-Grade Advisement Program Parent Letter

Dear Parents:

We invite you and your child to attend an individual advisement session with a faculty adviser concerning your son's or daughter's schedule for the next school year at _____ High School. The school's faculty and staff believe this individual advisement session to be an important step in each student's success at the high school level. The adviser will follow the agenda below during the advisement session:

- Review the student's academic record
- Review the student's attendance record
- Review current teacher recommendations
- Discuss the student's career goals and plans
- Address parent and student questions and concerns
- Assist the student to select an appropriate program of study
- Assist the student to develop an appropriate six-year educational plan
- Select courses for next school year

Enclosed is an information packet that describes the programs of study and course offerings available at _____ High School. A registration form and an appointment request have been included in the packet and must be completed and returned to _____ (name) by _____ (date). All advisement appointments will be held in the _____ at _____ High School.

We look forward to meeting with you and your child.

Sincerely,
School Faculty and Staff

FORM 2.18B

Rising Ninth-Grade Advisement Program Appointment Request

Directions:

Please review the information below and mark your preferred appointment dates and times (indicate 1st, 2nd, and 3rd choice). **PLEASE RETURN THE APPOINTMENT REQUEST TO _____ BY _____.** A staff member from the high school will call to confirm your appointment information.

APPOINTMENT REQUEST

Student Name: _____

Current Middle School: _____

Homeroom Teacher: _____

Parent Name: _____

Home Telephone Number: _____

Best time/number to call during the day to confirm appointment time: _____

<u>**Advisement Dates:**</u>

☐ _____ (Monday)   ☐ _____ (Tuesday)   ☐ _____ (Wednesday)

☐ _____ (Thursday)   ☐ _____ (Friday)

<u>**Advisement Times:**</u>

☐ _____ AM   ☐ _____ AM   ☐ _____ AM   ☐ _____ AM

☐ _____ AM   ☐ _____ AM   ☐ _____ AM   ☐ _____ AM

☐ _____ PM   ☐ _____ PM   ☐ _____ PM   ☐ _____ PM

☐ _____ PM   ☐ _____ P M   ☐ _____ PM   ☐ _____ PM

FORM 2.19

Rising Ninth-Grade Advisement Program

Adviser's Conference Schedule

Adviser's Name: _____   Conference Date: _____

TIME	STUDENT NAME	PARENT NAME	TELEPHONE NUMBER

FORM 2.20

Rising Ninth-Grade Advisement Program
Adviser's Schedule Change

Adviser's Name: _____

Please: ☐ ADD   ☐ DELETE

STUDENT NAME	CONFERENCE DATE	CONFERENCE TIME

FORM 2.21

Rising Ninth-Grade Advisement Program Conference Agenda

Student Name: _____ Conference Date: _____

Parent Name: _____

Current Mailing Address: _____

Home Telephone: _____ Work Telephone: _____

_____ 1. Greetings and introductions

_____ 2. Explain objectives of conference

_____ 3. Discuss current school profile

_____ 4. Review graduation requirements for class of _____

     _____ Explain/Discuss the different pathways/diploma choices

     _____ Review total number of credits required for each program of study

     _____ Explain/Define core courses

     _____ Review core requirements for each diploma program

     _____ Discuss sequence of core courses

     _____ Discuss all tests required for high school graduation

_____ 5. Review/Discuss the student's academic history (last report card grades and attendance)

_____ 6. Review/Discuss four- to six-year program planning:

     _____ Discuss selecting a program of study

     _____ Review the areas of concentration offered at the high school

     _____ Review postsecondary options (four-year college and/or technical college)

Note: Student's program of study selection should lead into his or her next two years of postsecondary education.

_____ 7. Review/Complete student's registration form

_____ 8. Discuss extracurricular programs and activities offered at the high school

_____ 9. Address parent and student concerns

_____ 10. RETURN THE FOLLOWING ITEMS TO THE STUDENT'S ADVISEMENT FOLDER: Advisement Conference Agenda Checklist, Student Registration Form, and Student Report Card

FORM 2.22

Rising Ninth-Grade Advisement Program Parent Survey

The Counseling Staff needs your assistance in assessing our Rising Individual Advisement Program. Please complete the survey below by circling the response that best depicts your experience during your advisement session. This survey looks at various components of the session and the results will assist the staff in determining how effective the Rising Ninth-Grade Advisement Program was for you and your student. Please write any additional comments on the back of the survey. Please fold and place the completed form in the evaluation box.
THANK YOU!

5 strongly agree   4 agree   3 undecided   2 disagree   1 strongly disagree

CIRCLE ONE NUMBER FOR EACH STATEMENT

1. The adviser began the appointment on time.   5   4   3   2   1

2. The adviser was friendly and professional.   5   4   3   2   1

3. The adviser used language that was easy to understand.   5   4   3   2   1

4. The adviser reviewed my son's or daughter's current academic progress.   5   4   3   2   1

5. The adviser discussed my son's or daughter's career interests.   5   4   3   2   1

6. The adviser reviewed the programs of study offered at the high school.   5   4   3   2   1

7. The adviser reviewed the program requirements for graduation.   5   4   3   2   1

8. The adviser reviewed information on standardized tests (PSAT, SAT, ACT, ASSET, ASVAB, and/or AP).   5   4   3   2   1

9. The adviser assisted my son or daughter to develop a six-year educational plan and select courses for the next school year.   5   4   3   2   1

10. The adviser provided information about the school's tutorial services and programs.   5   4   3   2   1

11. The adviser provided information about summer or night school programs.   5   4   3   2   1

12. The individual advisement session was productive and helped me to better understand what my son or daughter is doing to prepare for high school and postsecondary experiences.   5   4   3   2   1

Best Practice 3

Design and Implement an Extensive Career Education Program

Best Practice 3: Design and Implement an Extensive Career Education Program

Counselors must implement programs and provide resources that facilitate the career development of all middle and high school students. Students need assistance to develop the essential skills for making informed career decisions and developing beliefs, values, skills, and knowledge of the world of work. School counselors must familiarize themselves with career research and information from sources such as the National Career Development Guidelines, the U.S. Department of Education's 16 Career Clusters, and the Secretary's Commission on Achieving Necessary Skill (SCANS) in order to build solid programs that prepare students for success in the modern workplace. Career education programs should have a school-to-career focus and provide students with opportunities to gain occupational experiences through internships, employer mentoring, and career shadowing programs. Counselors must assist students to develop an understanding of the relationships among educational achievement, career training, and job placement. The goal of an extensive career education program is to lay the foundation for lifelong career development and facilitate the successful transition of students to their postsecondary endeavors.

In the first half of this chapter, we review the basic principles of career development and provide a practical guide for designing an extensive career education program and implementing a step-by-step career development plan for middle and high school students. In the second half of the chapter, we identify career resource centers and career portfolios as essential tools for promoting career development. We describe how to design an effective career resource center and list the materials and equipment that are essential to a center's daily operation. We then review the purpose of student career portfolios and provide information that supports the practice. Finally, the Forms and Supplemental Resources in this chapter provide a wealth of career information and samples of technology-connected career lesson plans.

SECTION 1: BASIC PRINCIPLES OF CAREER DEVELOPMENT

ASCA (2003) defines career development as "the necessary skills and attitudes for successful transition from school to work or postsecondary training or education" (p. 129). ASCA's National Standards (Competencies and Indicators) include three broad standards of career development:

- Students will acquire the skills to investigate the world of work in relation to knowledge of self and to make informed career decisions.
- Students will employ strategies to achieve future career goals with success and satisfaction.
- Students will understand the relationship between personal qualities, education, training, and the world of work. (pp. 83–84)

To implement the first standard, school counselors must develop activities and programs that promote career awareness and employment readiness. The second standard requires the implementation of career information strategies and the identification of career goals. The third standard involves acquiring necessary knowledge and using skills to achieve career goals. The ASCA National Model provides an excellent means for the secondary school counselor to plan a developmental program for students.

To be effective in planning, implementing, and evaluating career development programs, one needs to be aware of the significant factors in career planning. Certainly, intellectual ability is a key factor in educational and career choice. Suppose a student entered an occupation in which most of the workers had a higher level of intellectual functioning; he or she would be at a distinct disadvantage in terms of competing for work. On the other hand, suppose the student entered a career in which most of the workers were at a lower level of intellectual ability; he or she may be bored and unchallenged by the lack of competition. Other factors include aptitudes, interests, gender differences, environmental influences, and personal preferences.

Intellectual ability and aptitudes are important in making career decisions because a person needs to be able to do the work required in his or her chosen occupation. In terms of preparing for a specific career, the student must be able to gain admission into the school, college, or program that prepares individuals for that occupation. Often, after completing a preparation program, the potential worker must pass a competency test, certification process, or a licensing procedure to be able to practice in a particular career. Also, in some cases, a student must possess certain physical competencies to be able to meet the demands of an occupation. For example, an individual may be accepted into dental school based on a history of excellent achievement and ability but not be able to complete the program in dentistry because of poor manual dexterity. Students need to be aware and understand the importance of intellectual ability and implementation of aptitudes in career planning.

Personality and personal preferences certainly play an important role in career planning. It appears that certain individuals are unsuited to particular occupations due to personality (Shertzer & Stone, 1971, p. 341). Personality, personal preferences, interests, and self-concept are interrelated, and each factor has a significant impact on the other. Holland's theory of career development readily employs personality factors as key determinants of occupational choice. Holland assumed that occupational choice is an "expression of personality and members of the same occupation share similar personality characteristics" (Shertzer & Stone, p. 342). However, the school counselor must be cautious in using personality adjustment inventories in his or her career guidance programs since there is a problem with students faking responses. Also, values and attitudes in various subgroups of student populations may affect the outcome of student responses on these instruments. Personal preferences, such as work-related values and educational goals, have an impact upon career decisions. These values include respect, prestige, money, creativity, responsibility, security, and altruism. The student examines the potential career to determine if these or other important values are being met in the occupation. Of course, the student must also consider the number of years of education or training he plans to obtain. Some individuals only desire to continue their education for a year or two after high school, thus eliminating jobs that require longer periods of preparation.

As the ASCA model indicates, it is very worthwhile for students to be able to understand the relationship among personal qualities, education and training, and the world of work. For the career planning process to be effective, abilities, interests, values, education and training, and specific career requirements need to mesh. The Occu-Scan materials in the Armed Services Vocational Aptitude Battery's *Exploring Careers* workbook are effective for showing students this process (U.S. Military Entrance Processing Command, 1998). Using a concrete, hands-on approach, this workbook assists students to apply the criteria of interests, abilities, aptitudes, values, and education to career planning.

SECTION 2: DESIGN APPROPRIATE CAREER DEVELOPMENT PLANS FOR MIDDLE AND HIGH SCHOOL STUDENTS

The school counselor must understand and adapt the National Career Development Guidelines to design a successful career development plan at the middle and high school levels (*The National Career Development Guidelines*, n.d.). Under the guidelines, competencies and strategies are listed in three broad areas: self-knowledge, educational and occupational exploration, and career planning. In the career development process, the student is answering the following questions: Who am I? Where am I going? How am I going to get there?

Competencies under the self-knowledge strand include information and skills about the importance of a positive self-concept, appropriate ways to interact with others, and the significance of growth and change in life. In the educational and occupational strand, competencies include the importance of educational achievement to career choices; the relationship between work and learning; the skills needed to locate, evaluate, and use career information; and the skills necessary to seek, obtain, and keep jobs. Career planning competencies relate to decision-making skills, the inter-relationship of life roles, changing gender roles in various occupations, and the career planning process. The school counselor develops activities and strategies so students can gain knowledge and skills in these areas. In implementing these strategies, a comprehensive career program that meets the needs of the students is developed.

After investigating the National Career Development Guidelines and establishing the appropriate competencies and strategies for a career development program, the next step is to organize the supporting activities by grade level. The plan ought to include objectives, activities and personnel responsible for the activities, the materials needed, and the means of evaluation. For example, under the career planning strand, the objective may be to administer a career interest survey to all ninth graders to determine their measured career work interests. The activity would be to have students access the O'Net Interest Profile available on the Internet in the computer lab to measure their career interests and relate them to specific occupations. The career center specialist would be responsible for implementing the activity, and the students would complete an evaluation form listing their top two interest areas and four related occupations.

The next two steps in designing a career development program are research and validation. To implement the program and keep it running smoothly, attention must be paid to activities, resources, and materials. The computer and the Internet are great assets for these steps. A continual process of investigation is necessary to keep the most current and accurate information available to the students. Also, it is important that the activities and materials be presented in a creative manner. For example, career fairs are an excellent way to inform students of occupations. A new twist to that would be to have specialized career fairs, such as a "Transportation Day" at which workers who use a vehicle in their jobs bring them to the school parking lot. The students could then learn about the careers first-hand by exploring the different vehicles and talking with the drivers. In addition, the program ought to be sound and meet the ASCA National Standards or the National Career Development Guidelines.

Finally, the school counselor must be a leader in designing and implementing a career development program at the middle and high school levels. The education and training of counselors gives them the skills and knowledge necessary to play an important role in the development of a career program for all students. We have created a basic career development plan template and provide a sample career development plan for grades 9–12.

The following forms are found in this section:

Form 3.1 Career Development Plan

Form 3.2 Job Shadowing Application

Form 3.3 Internship Application

SECTION 3: DESIGN AND IMPLEMENT A COMPREHENSIVE CAREER CENTER

School counselors are often in search of strategies that will assist and support their efforts to effectively implement a comprehensive career development program. A Career Center is a tool that school counselors can use to facilitate the process of career exploration and development for all students. The primary goals of a Career Center in an educational setting are to assist students to develop the essential skills for making informed educational and career decisions, prepare students to meet the changing demands of the twenty-first century workforce, facilitate student transitions to postsecondary experiences, and lay the foundation for lifelong learning and career planning. According to Schutt (1999),

> Centers should seek to contribute to the students' career development by
>
> - teaching students the skills necessary to answer the three primary questions (Who am I?, Where am I going?, and How do I get there?) when they are developmentally ready to learn and use them,
> - helping faculty connect course material to the world of work,
> - strengthening critical career development competency areas by having students apply their knowledge and skills to increasingly complex situations. (pp. 95–96)

A school's Career Center is a resource that can be used by the entire school community. According to Feller (1998),

> A comprehensive Career Center in the high school provides reference materials for students to personally research various careers and the training required for those careers. Teachers can find information to use in developing classroom activities to help build skills, competencies, and knowledge of careers that will better prepare graduates for employment and continuous education. (p. 1)

At the middle school level, Schutt (1999) states that Career Centers should

- continue to educate students, school staff, and parents about the career development process,
- publicize the career development resources available in the center to parents and school staff,
- teach students about the many strategies for accessing information and the connections between the information databases,
- work with students to increase skills in the areas of managing information and planning,
- support efforts to get students involved in workplace simulation activities or actual work sites, and
- guide students in the creation of a career development portfolio. (p. 88)

We have fashioned a Career Center model for secondary schools based on the One-Stop Career Center model developed by the United States Department of Labor in keeping with the *Workforce Investment Act* of 1998. The basic framework of our model includes both a self-service and direct service delivery system. This system mirrors the core and intensive service components of the Department of Labor's One-Stop Career Center. Often, students only need access to information, resource materials, computers, and other tools in order to facilitate their explorations; however, secondary students need direct instruction and assistance as they begin to seek answers to the "Who," "Where," and "How" questions. The remainder of this section provides general steps for developing a Career Center and lists the basic materials and equipment that are essential to a Center's daily operation. On a final note, we emphasize that a Career Center is a resource that can be implemented with minimum cost but can yield pinnacle results.

Steps for Designing a Career Center

1. Formulate a Career Center study committee.
   a. The committee must be composed of representatives of the school community.
   b. The committee must be limited to a manageable number and meet regularly.
   c. The committee will serve as an advisory board once the Career Center is in place.

2. Establish the need for a Career Center.
   a. Survey the school's stakeholders.
   b. Survey the local businesses and industries.
   c. Review school data (high school graduation rate, attendance to postsecondary institutions, follow-up studies with graduates).
   d. Collect, analyze, and evaluate data and write a needs statement for the Career Center.

3. Develop a Beliefs and Mission Statement for the Career Center.
   a. The set of beliefs provides direction for the Career Center and lays the foundation for the Center's Mission Statement.
   b. The Mission Statement must provide a clear vision for the Career Center and clearly state the role the Center will play in the careers and educational development of all students.

4. Write specific goals and objectives for the Career Center.
   a. A goal is a general statement outlining what students will be able to do as a result of a strategy or intervention.
   b. An objective is a specific statement describing student actions or performances to be exhibited in order to achieve mastery of a designated goal.

5. Establish personnel requirements.
   a. Establish a title for the position (e.g., Career Specialist).
   b. Develop roles and responsibilities for the Career Specialist.
   c. Develop personnel selection criteria (certified or noncertified, level of education, years of experience, etc.).

6. Establish policies and procedures for the Career Center.
   a. Policies are rules and regulations that pertain to the Career Center's function and daily operation.
   b. Procedures are methods or courses of action that state how a specific policy is to be carried out.

7. Select the Career Center location and general characteristics.
   a. The Career Center should be in a central location in the school (i.e., easily accessible for all students).
   b. The Career Center should have a welcoming appearance.
   c. The Career Center's materials should be organized and readily accessible to students, parents, teachers, and staff members.
   d. The Career Center should provide tables or individual desks for students to review materials in a leisurely manner and provide enough room to navigate from the various stations (computer, video, printed materials, etc.).

8. Select the Career Center materials.
   a. The Career Center must contain a wide variety of career and educational resources.
   b. The Career Center's resources must be available in the form of books, magazines, computer programs, videos, and other formats.
   c. A Career Center should have computers with Internet capability, a television, a VCR and DVD player, several tape players/recorders, and other equipment necessary to assist students.
   d. A LCD projector and laptop computer are recommended in order for the Career Specialist to work more effectively with groups of students.
   e. The Career Specialist must build a list of business partners that are willing to provide students with job shadowing or internship opportunities, serve as mentors to students pursuing particular

career interests, and provide feedback about the needs of the business community.

    f. All the Career Center's materials must be updated or reviewed yearly (Inventory).

9. Develop and maintain the Career Center Web Page (suggested page contents below).

    a. Meet your Career Specialist

        i. Picture (use digital camera)
        ii. Biography

    b. Career Specialist duties and areas of responsibility
    c. Career Specialist's contact information

        i. Telephone numbers with extensions
        ii. E-mail addresses

    d. Career Center information

        i. Career Center's hours of operation
        ii. Career Center's purpose
        iii. Career Center's goals and objectives
        iv. Student appointments with the Career Specialist

    e. Parent and student information and resources

        i. Specific grade level information
        ii. Monthly Career Center bulletin (noting important dates and upcoming events; specific college, career, and grade level information; character word of the month; and other tidbits)
        iii. Monthly calendar of events
        iv. Special programs information (job shadowing, internship, etc.)
        v. Part-time employment information
        vi. College and career information (to include college and career fair information)
        vii. College visits information
        viii. Financial aid information
        ix. A listing of college representatives

    f. Scholarship bulletin
    g. Web site links

        i. College
        ii. Financial aid and scholarships
        iii. Career
        iv. Career information for specific fields
        v. College entrance exams

10. Develop a data collection and evaluation plan.

    a. The Career Center committee will devise the plan.
    b. The Career Specialist will maintain a daily log sheet and complete a monthly report.

c. The Career Specialist will maintain a suggestion box and review and adjust the program based on major concerns of the school's stakeholders.

d. The Career Specialist will administer a needs assessment to the school community at the end of each school year.

SECTION 4: CAREER PORTFOLIOS FOR STUDENTS

A career portfolio is an excellent tool that students can use to document their journeys through the career development process. A student's portfolio should contain information pertaining to self-assessment, document career exploration efforts, highlight skills and experience, showcase exemplary student products or projects, and reveal student personal reflections. According to Wonacott (2001),

> Career portfolios provide evidence of individuals' knowledge and skills in working with data, people, and things. Developing a portfolio can be a valuable career awareness and career planning activity for youth, including those with special needs, and adults; a productive instructional activity involving critical reflection and analytical thinking; and a very useful tool in job search and career change. (p. 1)

We suggest that career portfolios for secondary students contain, at a minimum, the information listed below, organized in an uncomplicated manner. Students' career portfolios may be maintained in a folder or in a three-ring binder. This information is best kept in a secure location at the school in order to ensure that students update the information regularly. In addition, the format should be revised based on students' needs.

Career Portfolio Contents

- Student résumé
- Documentation of skills and abilities
- School awards and honors
- Memberships in school clubs and organizations (note any offices held)
- Interest inventories
- Program of study and courses completed (transcript)
- Work experience (note all job shadowing, internship, and part-time job experiences)
- Hobbies
- Showcase products or projects
- Career goals
- Letters of recommendation or references

The following forms are found in this section:

Resource 3.1: Overview of Career Development Resources

Resource 3.2: National Career Development Guidelines: Middle/ Junior High School Student Competencies and Indicators

Resource 3.3: National Career Development Guidelines: High School Student Competencies and Indicators

Resource 3.4: U.S. Department of Education 16 Career Clusters

Resource 3.5: The Secretary's Commission on Achieving Necessary Skills (SCANS): A Three-Part Foundation of Skills and Personal Qualities

Resource 3.6: The Secretary's Commission on Achieving Necessary Skills (SCANS): SCANS Five Competencies

Resource 3.7: Sample Career Center Newsletter

Resource 3.8: Sample Technology-Connected Career Lesson Plans

Resource 3.9: Recommended Career Center References and Resources

RESOURCE 3.1

Overview of Career Development Resources

1. National Career Development Guidelines

The National Career Development Guidelines is one of several initiatives that support the expansion of state career development capacity and comprehensive competency-based career guidance programs in various local programs. This initiative, sponsored by the National Occupational Information Coordinating Committee (NOICC), has provided leverage funding to states to support the development and improvement of comprehensive career development programs. It has combined with other program improvement incentives such as Carl D. Perkins Vocational Education Act funds, state efforts to develop goals and models for career guidance, and local interest in making guidance more accountable and programmatic. Over forty states have used the National Career Development Guidelines as part of a comprehensive statewide strategy (Miller, 1992, p. 1).

According to Lankard (1991), the National Career Development Guidelines provide a comprehensive program that will lead students of all ages through a sequential program of career development (p. 1).

2. U.S. Department of Education 16 Career Clusters

The Career Clusters Initiative began in 1996 as the Building Linkages Initiative and was a collaborative effort between the U.S. Department of Education, the Office of Vocational and Adult Education (OVAE), the National School-to-Work Office (NSTWO), and the National Skill Standards Board (NSSB). The purpose of the Initiative was to establish linkages among state educational agencies, secondary and postsecondary educational institutions, employers, industry groups, other stakeholders, and federal agencies. The goal was to create curricular frameworks, in broad career clusters, designed to prepare students to transition successfully from high school to postsecondary education or employment in a career area, or both (U.S. Department of Education, 2000, p. 3).

3. The Secretary's Commission on Achieving Necessary Skills

The Secretary's Commission on Achieving Necessary Skills (SCANS) was asked to define the skills needed for employment; propose acceptable levels of proficiency; suggest effective ways to assess proficiency; and develop a dissemination strategy for the nation's schools, businesses, and homes. In addition, the Commission examined the demands of the workplace and whether today's young people are capable of meeting those demands. The SCANS identified five competencies and a three-part foundation of skills and personal qualities that are essential for solid job performance.

RESOURCE 3.2

National Career Development Guidelines: Middle/Junior High School Student Competencies and Indicators

Area of Career Development: Self-Knowledge

Competency I: Knowledge of the influence of a positive self-concept.

Indicators:

Describe personal likes and dislikes.

Describe individual skills required to fulfill different life roles.

Describe how one's behavior influences the feelings and actions of others.

Identify environmental influences on attitudes, behaviors, and aptitudes.

Competency II: Skills to interact with others.

Indicators:

Demonstrate respect for the feelings and beliefs of others.

Demonstrate an appreciation for the similarities and differences among people.

Demonstrate tolerance and flexibility in interpersonal and group situations.

Demonstrate skills in responding to criticism.

Demonstrate effective group membership skills.

Demonstrate effective social skills.

Demonstrate understanding of different cultures, lifestyles, attitudes, and abilities.

Competency III: Knowledge of the importance of growth and change.

Indicators:

Identify feelings associated with significant experiences.

Identify internal and external sources of stress.

Demonstrate ways of responding to others when under stress.

Describe changes that occur in the physical, psychological, social, and emotional development of an individual.

Describe physiological and psychological factors as they relate to career development.

Describe the importance of career, family, and leisure activities to mental, emotional, physical, and economic well-being.

Area of Career Development: Educational and Occupational Exploration

Competency IV: Knowledge of the benefits of educational achievement to career opportunities.

Indicators:

Describe the importance of academic and occupational skills in the work world.

Identify how the skills taught in school subjects are used in various occupations.

Describe individual strengths and weaknesses in school subjects.

Describe a plan of action for increasing basic educational skills.

Describe the skills needed to adjust to changing occupational requirements.

Describe how continued learning enhances the ability to achieve goals.

Describe how skills relate to the selection of high school courses of study.

Describe how aptitudes and abilities relate to broad occupational groups.

Competency V: Understanding the relationship between work and learning.

Indicators:

Demonstrate effective learning habits and skills.

Demonstrate an understanding of the importance of personal skills and attitudes to job success.

Describe the relationship of personal attitudes, beliefs, abilities, and skills to occupations.

Competency VI: Skills to locate, understand, and use career information.

Indicators:

Identify various ways that occupations can be classified.

Identify a number of occupational groups for exploration.

Demonstrate skills in using school and community resources to learn about occupational groups.

Identify sources to obtain information about occupational groups, including self-employment.

Identify skills that are transferable from one occupation to another.

Identify sources of employment in the community.

Competency VII: Knowledge of skills necessary to seek and obtain jobs.

Indicators:

Demonstrate personal qualities (e.g., dependability, punctuality, getting along with others) that are needed to get and keep jobs.

Describe terms and concepts used in describing employment opportunities and conditions.

Demonstrate skills to complete a job application.

Demonstrate skills and attitudes essential for a job interview.

Competency VIII: Understanding of how work relates to the needs and functions of the economy and society.

Indicators:

Describe the importance of work to society.

Describe the relationship between work and economic and societal needs.

Describe the economic contributions workers make to society.

Describe the effects that societal, economic, and technological changes have on occupations.

Area of Career Development: Career Planning

Competency IX: Skills to make decisions.

Indicators:

Describe personal beliefs and attitudes.

Describe how career development is a continuous process with series of choices.

Identify possible outcomes of decisions.

Describe school courses related to personal, educational, and occupational interests.

Describe how the expectations of others affect career planning.

Identify ways in which decisions about education and work relate to other major life decisions.

Identify advantages and disadvantages of various secondary and post-secondary programs for the attainment of career goals.

Identify the requirements for secondary and postsecondary programs.

Competency X: Knowledge of the interrelationship of life roles.

Indicators:

Identify how different work and family patterns require varying kinds and amounts of energy, participation, motivation, and talent.

Identify how work roles at home satisfy needs of the family.

Identify personal goals that may be satisfied through a combination of work, community, social, and family roles.

Identify personal leisure choices in relation to lifestyle and the attainment of future goals.

Describe advantages and disadvantages of various life role options.

Describe the interrelationships between family, occupational, and leisure decisions.

Competency XI: Knowledge of different occupations and changing male/female roles.

Indicators:

Describe advantages and problems of entering nontraditional occupations.

Describe the advantages of taking courses related to personal interest, even if they are most often taken by members of the opposite gender.

Describe stereotypes, biases, and discriminatory behaviors that may limit opportunities for women and men in certain occupations.

Competency XII: Understanding the process of career planning.

Indicators:

Demonstrate knowledge of exploratory processes and programs.

Identify school courses that meet tentative career goals.

Demonstrate knowledge of academic and vocational programs offered at the high school level.

Describe skills needed in a variety of occupations, including self-employment.

Identify strategies for managing personal resources (e.g., talents, time, money) to achieve tentative career goals.

Develop an individual career plan, updating information from the elementary-level plan and including tentative decisions to be implemented in high school.

RESOURCE 3.3

National Career Development Guidelines: High School Student Competencies and Indicators

Area of Career Development: Self-Knowledge

Competency I: Understanding the influence of a positive self-concept.

Indicators:

Identify and appreciate personal interests, abilities, and skills.

Demonstrate the ability to use peer feedback.

Demonstrate an understanding of how individual characteristics relate to achieving personal, social, educational, and career goals.

Demonstrate an understanding of environmental influences on one's behaviors.

Demonstrate an understanding of the relationship between personal behavior and self-concept.

Competency II: Skills to interact positively with others.

Indicators:

Demonstrate effective interpersonal skills.

Demonstrate interpersonal skills required for working with and for others.

Describe appropriate employer and employee interactions in various situations.

Demonstrate how to express feelings, reactions, and ideas in an appropriate manner.

Competency III: Understanding the impact of growth and development.

Indicators:

Describe how developmental changes affect physical and mental health.

Describe the effect of emotional and physical health on career decisions.

Describe healthy ways of dealing with stress.

Demonstrate behaviors that maintain physical and mental health.

Area of Career Development: Educational and Occupational Exploration

Competency IV: Understanding the relationship between educational achievement and career planning.

Indicators:

Demonstrate how to apply academic and vocational skills to achieve personal goals.

Describe the relationship of academic and vocational skills to personal interests.

Describe how skills developed in academic and vocational programs relate to career goals.

Describe how education relates to the selection of college majors, further training, and/or entry into the job market.

Describe transferable skills that can apply to a variety of occupations and changing occupational requirements.

Describe how learning skills are required in the workplace.

Competency V: Understanding the need for positive attitudes toward work and learning.

Indicators:

Identify the positive contributions workers make to society.

Demonstrate knowledge of the social significance of various occupations.

Demonstrate a positive attitude toward work.

Demonstrate learning habits and skills that can be used in various educational situations.

Demonstrate positive work attitudes and behaviors.

Competency VI: Skills to locate, evaluate, and interpret career information.

Indicators:

Describe the educational requirements of various occupations.

Demonstrate the use of a range of resources (e.g., handbooks, career materials, labor market information, and computerized career information delivery systems).

Demonstrate knowledge of various classification systems that categorize occupations and industries (e.g., Dictionary of Occupational Titles).

Describe the concept of career ladders.

Describe the advantages and disadvantages of self-employment as a career option.

Identify individuals in selected occupations as possible information resources, role models, or mentors.

Describe the influence of change in supply and demand for workers in different occupations.

Identify how employment trends relate to education and training.

Describe the impact of factors such as population, climate, and geographic location on occupational opportunities.

Competency VII: Skills to prepare to seek, obtain, maintain, and change jobs.

Indicators:

Demonstrate skills to locate, interpret, and use information about job openings and opportunities.

Demonstrate academic or vocational skills required for a full or part-time job.

Demonstrate skills and behaviors necessary for a successful job interview.

Demonstrate skills in preparing a résumé and completing job applications.

Identify specific job openings.

Demonstrate employability skills necessary to obtain and maintain jobs.

Demonstrate skills to assess occupational opportunities (e.g., working conditions, benefits, and opportunities for change).

Describe placement services available to make the transition from high school to civilian employment, the armed services, or postsecondary education or training.

Demonstrate an understanding that job opportunities often require relocation.

Demonstrate skills necessary to function as a consumer and manage financial resources.

Competency VIII: Understanding how societal needs and functions influence the nature and structure of work.

Indicators:

Describe the effect of work on lifestyles.

Describe how society's needs and functions affect the supply of goods and services.

Describe how occupational and industrial trends relate to training and employment.

Demonstrate an understanding of the global economy and how it affects each individual.

Area of Career Development: Career Planning

Competency IX: Skills to make decisions.

Indicators:

Demonstrate responsibility for making tentative educational and occupational choices.

Identify alternatives in given decision-making situations.

Describe personal strengths and weaknesses in relationship to postsecondary education and training requirements.

Identify appropriate choices during high school that will lead to marketable skills for entry-level employment or advanced training.

Identify and complete required steps toward transition from high school to entry into postsecondary education and training programs or work.

Identify steps to apply for and secure financial assistance for postsecondary education and training.

Competency X: Understanding the interrelationship of life roles.

Indicators:

Demonstrate knowledge of life stages.

Describe factors that determine lifestyles (e.g., socioeconomic status, culture, values, occupational choices, work habits).

Describe ways in which occupational choices may affect lifestyle.

Describe the contribution of work to a balanced and productive life.

Describe ways in which work, family, and leisure roles are interrelated.

Describe different career patterns and their potential effect on family patterns and lifestyle.

Describe the importance of leisure activities.

Demonstrate ways that occupational skills and knowledge can be acquired through leisure.

Competency XI: Understanding the continuous changes in male/female roles.

Indicators:

Identify factors that have influenced the changing career patterns of women and men.

Identify evidence of gender stereotyping and bias in educational programs and occupational settings.

Demonstrate attitudes, behaviors, and skills that contribute to eliminating gender bias and stereotyping.

Identify courses appropriate to tentative occupational choices.

Describe the advantages and problems of nontraditional occupations.

Competency XII: Skills in career planning.

Indicators:

Describe career plans that reflect the importance of lifelong learning.

Demonstrate knowledge of postsecondary vocational and academic programs.

Demonstrate knowledge that changes may require retraining and upgrading of employees' skills.

Describe school and community resources to explore educational and occupational choices.

Describe the costs and benefits of self-employment.

Demonstrate occupational skills developed through volunteer experiences, part-time employment, or cooperative education programs.

Demonstrate skills necessary to compare education and job opportunities.

Develop an individual career plan, updating information from earlier plans and including tentative decisions to be implemented after high school.

RESOURCE 3.4

U.S. Department of Education 16 Career Clusters

1. Agricultural, Food, and Natural Resources

The production, processing, marketing, distribution, financing, and development of agricultural commodities and resources including food, fiber, wood products, natural resources, horticulture, and other plant and animal products and resources.

2. Architecture and Construction

Careers in designing, planning, managing, building, and maintaining the built environment.

3. Arts, A/V Technology, and Communications

Designing, producing, exhibiting, performing, writing, and publishing multimedia content including visual and performing arts and design, journalism, and entertainment services.

4. Business Management and Administration

Business management and administration careers encompass planning, organizing, directing, and evaluating business functions essential to efficient and productive business operations. Business management and administration career opportunities are available in every sector of the economy.

5. Education and Training

Planning, managing, and providing education and training services and related learning support services.

6. Finance

Planning services for financial and investment planning, banking, insurance, and business financial management.

7. Government and Public Administration

Executing governmental functions including governance; national security; foreign service; planning; revenue and taxation; regulation; and management and administration at the local, state, and federal levels.

8. Health Science

Planning, managing, and providing therapeutic services, diagnostic services, health informatics, support services, and biotechnology research and development.

9. Hospitality and Tourism

Hospitality and tourism encompasses the management, marketing, and operations of restaurants and other food services, lodging, attractions, recreation events, and travel-related services.

10. Human Services

Preparing individuals for employment in career pathways that relate to families and human needs.

11. Information Technology

Building linkages in IT occupations framework: for entry-level, technical, and professional careers related to the design, development, support, and management of hardware, software, multimedia, and systems integration services.

12. Law, Public Safety, and Security

Planning, managing, and providing legal, public safety, protective services, and homeland security, including professional and technical support services.

13. Manufacturing

Planning, managing, and performing the processing of materials into intermediate or final products and related professional and technical support activities such as production planning and control, maintenance and manufacturing, and process engineering.

14. Marketing, Sales, and Service

Planning, managing, and performing marketing activities to reach organizational objectives.

15. Science, Technology, Engineering, and Mathematics

Planning, managing, and providing scientific research and professional and technical services (e.g., physical science, social science, engineering) including laboratory and testing services and research and development services.

16. Transportation, Distribution, and Logistics

Planning, management, and movement of people, materials, and goods by road, pipeline, air, rail, and water and related professional and technical support services such as transportation infrastructure planning and management, logistics services, mobile equipment, and facility maintenance.

RESOURCE 3.5

The Secretary's Commission on Achieving Necessary Skills (SCANS): A Three-Part Foundation of Skills and Personal Qualities

1. **Basic Skills**: Reads, writes, performs arithmetic and mathematical operations, listens, and speaks

   A. Reading
   Locates, understands, and interprets written information in prose and in documents such as manuals, graphs, and schedules

   B. Writing
   Communicates thoughts, ideas, information, and messages in writing and creates documents such as letters, directions, manuals, reports, graphs, and flow charts

   C. Arithmetic/Mathematics
   Performs basic computations and approaches practical problems by choosing appropriately from a variety of mathematical techniques

   D. Listening
   Receives, attends to, interprets, and responds to verbal messages and other cues

   E. Speaking
   Organizes ideas and communicates orally

2. **Thinking Skills**: Thinks creatively, makes decisions, solves problems, visualizes, knows how to learn, and reasons

   A. Creative Thinking
   Generates new ideas

   B. Decision Making
   Specifies goals and constraints, generates alternatives, considers risks, and evaluates and chooses best alternative

   C. Problem Solving
   Recognizes problems and devises and implements plan of action

   D. Seeing Things in the Mind's Eye
   Organizes and processes symbols, pictures, graphs, objects, and other information

   E. Knowing How to Learn
   Uses efficient learning techniques to acquire and apply new knowledge and skills

F. Reasoning
Discovers a rule or principle underlying the relationship between two or more objects and applies it when solving a problem

3. **Personal Qualities:** Displays responsibility, self-esteem, sociability, self-management, and integrity and honesty

A. Responsibility
Exerts a high level of effort and perseveres towards goal attainment

B. Self-Esteem
Believes in own self-worth and maintains a positive view of self

C. Sociability
Demonstrates understanding, friendliness, adaptability, empathy, and politeness in group settings

D. Self-Management
Assesses self accurately, sets personal goals, monitors progress, and exhibits self-control

E. Integrity/Honesty
Chooses ethical courses of action

Source: U.S. Department of Labor, 1991, p. 12.

DEFINITIONS: THE FOUNDATION

Basic Skills

- Reading

Locates, understands, and interprets written information in prose and documents—including manuals, graphs, and schedules—to perform tasks; learns from text by determining the main idea or essential message; identifies relevant details, facts, and specifications; infers or locates the meaning of unknown or technical vocabulary; and judges the accuracy, appropriateness, style, and plausibility of reports, proposals, or theories of other writers.

- Writing

Communicates thoughts, ideas, information, and messages in writing; records information completely and accurately; composes and creates documents such as letters, directions, manuals, reports, proposals, graphs, flow charts; uses language, style, organization, and format appropriate to the subject matter, purpose, and audience. Includes supporting documentation and attends to level of detail; checks, edits, and revises for correct information, appropriate emphasis, form, grammar, spelling, and punctuation.

- Arithmetic

Performs basic computations; uses basic numerical concepts such as whole numbers and percentages in practical situations; makes reasonable estimates of arithmetic results without a calculator; and uses tables, graphs, diagrams, and charts to obtain or convey quantitative information.

- Mathematics

Approaches practical problems by choosing appropriately from a variety of mathematical techniques; uses quantitative data to construct logical explanations for real world situations; expresses mathematical ideas and concepts orally and in writing; and understands the role of chance in the occurrence and prediction of events.

- Listening

Receives, attends to, interprets, and responds to verbal messages and other cues, such as body language, in ways that are appropriate to the purpose, for example, to comprehend, to learn, to critically evaluate, to appreciate, or to support the speaker.

- Speaking

Organizes ideas and communicates oral messages appropriate to listeners and situations; participates in conversation, discussion, and group presentations; selects an appropriate medium for conveying a message; uses verbal languages and other cues such as body language appropriate in style, tone, and level of complexity to the audience and the occasion; speaks clearly and communicates message; understands and responds to listener feedback; and asks questions when needed.

Thinking Skills

- Creative Thinking

Uses imagination freely, combines ideas or information in new ways, makes connections between seemingly unrelated ideas, and reshapes goals in ways that reveal new possibilities.

- Decision Making

Specifies goals and constraints, generates alternatives, considers risks, and evaluates and chooses best alternatives.

- Problem Solving

Recognizes that a problem exists (i.e., there is a discrepancy between what is and what should or could be), identifies possible reasons for the discrepancy, and devises and implements a plan of action to resolve it. Evaluates and monitors progress and revises plan as indicated by findings.

- Seeing Things in the Mind's Eye

Organizes and processes symbols, pictures, graphs, objects, or other information; for example, seeing a building from blueprint, a system's operation from schematics, the flow of work activities from narrative descriptions, or the taste of food from reading a recipe.

- Knowing How to Learn

Recognizes and can use learning techniques to apply and adapt new knowledge and skills in both familiar and changing situations. Involves being aware of learning tools such as personal learning styles (visual, aural, etc.), formal learning strategies (note taking or clustering items that share some characteristics), and informal learning strategies (awareness of unidentified false assumptions that may lead to faulty conclusions).

- Reasoning

Discovers a rule or principle underlying the relationship between two or more objects and applies it in solving a problem. For example, uses logic to draw conclusions from available information, extracts rules or principles from a set of objects or written text, applies rules and principles to a new situation, or determines which conclusions are correct when given a set of facts and a set of conclusions.

Personal Qualities

- Responsibility

Exerts a high level of effort and perseverance towards goal attainment. Works hard to become excellent at doing tasks by setting high standards, paying attention to details, working well, and displaying a high level of concentration even when assigned an unpleasant task. Displays high standards of attendance, punctuality, enthusiasm, vitality, and optimism in approaching and completing tasks.

- Self-Esteem

Believes in own worth and maintains a positive view of self, demonstrates knowledge of own skills and abilities, is aware of impact on others, and knows own emotional capacity and needs and how to address them.

- Sociability

Demonstrates understanding, friendliness, adaptability, empathy, and politeness in new and ongoing group settings. Asserts self in familiar and unfamiliar social situations, relates well to others, responds appropriately as the situation requires, and takes an interest in what others say and do.

- Self-Management

Assesses own knowledge, skills, and abilities accurately; sets well-defined and realistic personal goals; monitors progress toward goal attainment and motivates self through goal achievement; exhibits self-control and responds to feedback unemotionally and non-defensively; is a "self-starter."

- Integrity/Honesty

Can be trusted. Recognizes when faced with making a decision or exhibiting behavior that may break with commonly-held personal or societal values; understands the impact of violating these beliefs and codes on an organization, self, and others; and chooses an ethical course of action.

Source: U.S. Department of Labor, 1991, pp. 46–47.

RESOURCE 3.6

The Secretary's Commission on Achieving Necessary Skills (SCANS): SCANS Five Competencies

1. **Resources:** Identifies, organizes, plans, and allocates resources
   A. Time
   Selects goal-related activities, ranks them, allocates time, and prepares and follows schedules

   B. Money
   Uses or prepares budgets, makes forecasts, keeps records, and makes appropriate adjustments to meet objectives

   C. Material and Facility
   Acquires, stores, allocates, and uses materials or space efficiently

   D. Human Resources
   Assesses skills and distributes work accordingly, evaluates performance, and provides feedback

2. **Interpersonal:** Works with others
   A. Participates as a Member of a Team
   Contributes to group effort

   B. Teaches Others New Skills

   C. Serves Clients/Customers
   Works to satisfy customers' expectations

   D. Exercises Leadership
   Communicates ideas to justify position, persuades and convinces others, responsibly challenges existing procedures and policies

   E. Negotiates
   Works toward agreements involving exchange of resources or resolving divergent interests

   F. Works with Cultural Diversity
   Works well with men and women and with a variety of ethnic, social, or educational backgrounds

3. **Information:** Acquires and uses information
   A. Acquires and Evaluates Information
   B. Organizes and Maintains Information
   C. Interprets and Communicates Information
   D. Uses Computers to Process Information

4. **Systems:** Understands complex interrelationships
   A. Understands Systems
   Knows how social, organizational, and technological systems work and operates effectively within them

B. Monitors and Corrects Performance
Distinguishes trends, predicts impact on system operations, diagnoses deviations in systems' performance, and corrects malfunctions

C. Improves and Designs Systems
Suggests modifications to existing systems and develops new or alternative systems to improve performance

5. **Technology:** Works with a variety of technologies
A. Selects Technology
Chooses procedures, tools, or equipment including computers and related technologies

B. Applies Technology to Task
Understands overall intent and proper procedures for setup and operation of equipment

C. Maintains and Troubleshoots Technology
Prevents, identifies, or solves problems with equipment, including computers and other technologies

Source: U.S. Department of Labor, 1991, p. 11.

DEFINITIONS: THE COMPETENCIES

Resources

- **Allocates Time.** Selects relevant, goal-related activities; ranks them in order of importance; allocates time to activities; and understands, prepares, and follows schedules.
- **Allocates Money.** Uses or prepares budgets (including making cost and revenue forecasts), keeps detailed records to track budget performance, and makes appropriate adjustments.
- **Allocates Material and Facility Resources.** Acquires, stores, and distributes materials, supplies, parts, equipment, space, or final products in order to make the best use of them.
- **Allocates Human Resources.** Assesses knowledge and skills and distributes work accordingly, evaluates performance, and provides feedback.

Interpersonal

- **Participates as a Member of a Team**. Works cooperatively with others and contributes to group with ideas, suggestions, and effort.
- **Teaches others**. Helps others learn.
- **Serves Clients/Customers**. Works and communicates with clients and customers to satisfy their expectations.
- **Exercises Leadership**. Communicates thoughts, feelings, and ideas to justify a position; encourages, persuades, convinces, or otherwise

motivates an individual or groups, including responsibly challenging existing procedures, policies, or authority.

- **Negotiates.** Works toward an agreement that may involve exchanging specific resources or resolving divergent interests.
- **Works with Cultural Diversity.** Works well with men and women and with a variety of ethnic, social, or educational backgrounds.

Information

- **Acquires and Evaluates Information.** Identifies need for data, obtains it from existing sources or creates it, and evaluates its relevance and accuracy.
- **Organizes and Maintains Information.** Organizes, processes, and maintains written or computerized records and other forms of information in a systematic fashion.
- **Interprets and Communicates Information.** Selects and analyzes information and communicates the results to others using oral, written, graphic, pictorial, or multimedia methods.
- **Uses Computers to Process Information.** Employs computers to acquire, organize, analyze, and communicate information.

Systems

- **Understands Systems.** Knows how social, organizational, and technological systems work and operates effectively within them.
- **Monitors and Corrects Performance.** Distinguishes trends, predicts impact of actions on system operations, diagnoses deviations in the function of a system or organization, and takes necessary action to correct performance.
- **Improves and Designs Systems.** Makes suggestions to modify existing systems to improve products or services and develops new or alternative systems.

Technology

- **Selects Technology.** Judges which set of procedures, tools, or machines, including computers and their programs, will produce the desired results.
- **Applies Technology to Task.** Understands the overall intent and the proper procedures for setting up and operating machines, including computers and their programming systems.
- **Maintains and Troubleshoots Technology.** Prevents, identifies, or solves problems in machines, computers, and other technologies.

Source: U.S. Department of Labor, 1991, p. 44–46.

RESOURCE 3.7

Sample Career Center Newsletter

 **Harlem High School**

The Career Center

Volume 1, Number 1 *Exploring Tomorrow Today!* December 2003

Upcoming Events

- HHS Financial Aid Workshop: Junior and Senior students and their parents.
- Date: 12/11/03
- Time: 7:00 P.M.

Ten Traps of Studying

1. *"I don't know where to begin."— Take control.*

2. *"I've got so much to study . . . and so little time."—Preview your work.*

3. *"This stuff is so dry, I can't even stay awake reading it."—Attack. Get involved.*

4. *"I read it. I understand it. But I just can't get it to sink in."—Elaborate. Remember the most meaningful sections of the material.*

5. *"I guess I understand it."—Test yourself. Make up questions.*

6. *"There's too much to remember."—Organize. Represent your work in an organized framework.*

7. *"I knew it a minute ago."—Review.*

8. *"But I like to study in bed."—Study in a physical location.*

9. *"Cramming before a test helps keep it fresh in my mind."—Spacing. Start studying now.*

10. *"I'm going to stay up all night 'til I get this." — Rest. Be alert for the test or class tomorrow.*

Final Exam Exemption Rules

9th, 10th, and 11th Grade
Students in grades nine, ten, and eleven with a course grade average of eighty or above with no absences from class; with a course average of eighty-five or above with no more than three absences from class; or with a course average of ninety or above, with no more than five absences, excused or prior approval, from class, and no disciplinary referrals that resulted in suspension, may exempt a maximum of two final examinations per semester. Students who meet the exemption criteria may choose the two examinations to be exempted. Students who meet the criteria for the semester may not exempt a final exam in the same content area as first semester.

12th Grade
Students in grade twelve with a course grade average of eighty or above and no absences from class, excused or prior approval; with a course average of eighty-five or above and with no more than three absences from class; or with a course average of ninety or above, with no more than five absences, excused or prior approval, from class and no disciplinary referrals that resulted in out-of-school suspension or in-school suspension may exempt all qualifying course examinations both semesters.

Phrase/Word of the Month

COMPASSION

College View

Campus Tours. Contact schools for more details.

Clark Atlanta University
Mon-Thurs 8 A.M.-8 P.M.
Friday 8 A.M.-5 P.M.
1-800-688-3228

Georgia College and State University
Mon-Fri 11:00 A.M.
Sat. 10:00 A.M.
1-800-342-0471

Important Dates

- SAT Test Date: 12/06/03

- SAT Registration Deadline for the January 24 Test Date: 12/22/03

- ACT Registration Deadline for the February 7 Test Date: 01/02/04

Scholarship

- Toyota Community Scholars Program Deadline: 12/05/03

- Burger King Deadline: 12/15/03

- Georgia Farm Bureau Field Services Deadline: 12/19/03

- Georgia State University Deadline: 01/01/04

Additional Information

- End of the course testing dates: December 1–12

- Semester Exams: December, 17, 18, and 19
Happy Holidays

'Tis the Season

The holidays are approaching; have you noticed the hustle and bustle in the shops? It seems all the stores are having "special sales" and people are taking advantage of these opportunities. To handle the increased volume, many stores have hired additional help. This is an opportunity to earn a little extra money for the holidays. Many individuals hope their temporary positions turn into permanent employment.

The Big Questions:
How many of those employed will still have the position after the holidays?
What characteristics did they demonstrate that helped them retain their position?

Quote or phrase . . .

The values we live by are worth more when we pass them on.

Oscar Wilde

RESOURCE 3.8

Sample Technology-Connected Career Lesson Plans

CORD (1999) suggests that the counselor's role in assisting students in career preparation includes providing groups of students with career information as well as individual career planning sessions (p. 18). It is important to use technology to provide students with the most current career information. Technology is a tool that not only engages the learner but also permits students to receive information upon demand, which facilitates the learning process. We have created five sample lesson plans that have been used with secondary school students in classroom guidance activities as part of a career development model. The plans follow a modified form of the Georgia State Department of Education's (1998) template and provide a structure for planning, implementing, managing, and evaluating the guidance activity (p. 29).

LESSON PLAN ONE

Title: Mapping Your Future: Occupations, Majors, and Schools

Subject/Topic Area: Guidance

Standards:

- Competency I: Understanding the influence of positive self-concept. Demonstrate an understanding of how individual characteristics relate to achieving personal, social, educational, and career goals.
- Competency IV: Understanding the relationship between educational achievement and career planning. Describe how education relates to the selection of college majors, further training, or entry into job market.
- Competency IX: Skills to make decisions. Demonstrate responsibility for making tentative educational and occupational choices.

Lesson Objectives:

1. Students will select three occupations of interest from the Georgia Career Information Center (GCIC) Web site and write three job briefs containing the following information: work activities, aptitudes, work setting, average entry level wages, preparation, and employment outlook.

2. Students will select an educational program of study related to one of their occupational interests and write a summary of the program overview, admission requirements, and typical course work.

3. Students will make choices of postsecondary schools by using the following selection categories: program of study, length of program, location of school, school size, admission requirements, and maximum tuition and fees.

4. Students will select three postsecondary schools that meet their selection criteria. (Students will use the GCIC Web site to meet these objectives.)

Technology Connection:

The senior English class meets in the computer lab and each student uses the Internet to reach the following site: www.gcic.peachnet.edu

Procedures:

As a behavior management strategy, students are given a red folded stock paper placard to be placed on the monitor when they have a question. The placards are numbered in repeating sets of four, so students may form groups to give summaries of their findings and report to the class. Each student is given a "Mapping Your Future" worksheet. The students access the Internet site and use the worksheet as their guide to complete the activity. As a culminating activity, the students meet in their groups to share their findings. The group selects a speaker to give the highlights of their search to the whole class. The worksheets are collected and students' names are checked on the class roster indicating that they returned their worksheets.

Assessment:

Large and small group participation and completion of the "Mapping Your Future" worksheet.

Materials/Technology Needed:

Red stock paper placards, Directions for Students, "Mapping Your Future" worksheet, computers in computer lab, and access to the Internet.

Related URLs:

www.usg.edu/ga-easy

LESSON PLAN 1 WORKSHEET

Mapping Your Future: Steps in Career and Education Planning

PERSONAL GUIDE FOR _____

(Student Name)

1. List three selected occupations from the **GCIS Web site.**

_____, _____,

_____

2. Complete the information below for each occupation you selected.

OCCUPATION 1:

    WORK ACTIVITIES:

    APTITUDES:

    WORK SETTING:

    AVERAGE ENTRY LEVEL WAGES:

    PREPARATION:

    EMPLOYMENT:

    EMPLOYMENT OUTLOOK:

OCCUPATION 2:

APTITUDES:

WORK SETTING:

AVERAGE ENTRY LEVEL WAGES:

PREPARATION:

EMPLOYMENT: AUGUSTA _____ GA _____ USA _____

EMPLOYMENT OUTLOOK:

OCCUPATION 3:

APTITUDES:

WORK SETTING:

AVERAGE ENTRY LEVEL WAGES:

PREPARATION:

EMPLOYMENT:

EMPLOYMENT OUTLOOK:

3. List your selected College or Technical College Program of Study.

Write a summary of the Program Overview:

Program Admission:

Typical Course Work:

Reference Source:

4. List Selection Categories for the School Sort.

Select Program

Length of Program

Location of School (Georgia)

School Size

Admission Requirements

Maximum Tuition and Fees

How many schools were listed?

List three of the schools.

Select one and list the following information about it:

Location: Student Enrollment:

Costs per year: List two student services:

5. List five things that you have learned from this lesson.

LESSON PLAN TWO

Title: Career Draw: First Job and Life on a Budget

Subject/Topic Area: Guidance: Career and Lifestyle Planning (11th Grade English Class)

Standards:

- Competency IV: Understanding the relationship between educational achievement and career planning. Describe how education is related to the selection of college majors, further training, or entry into the job market.
- Competency VI: Skills to locate, evaluate, and interpret career information. Demonstrate the use of a range of resources (e.g., handbooks, career materials, labor market information, and computerized career information delivery systems).
- Competency X: Understanding the interrelationship of life roles. Describe factors that determine lifestyles.

Lesson Objectives:

1. The students will identify the following information about their selected career: nature of the work, aptitudes needed for the career, work setting description, number of workers in Georgia and the Augusta area, average salary of workers, tools needed for job, and the preparation required for the job.

2. The students will select affordable housing and describe their lifestyle by completing the Budget Form worksheet.

3. The students will describe factors that determined their lifestyle in their oral presentations to the class.

Technology Connection:

Each section of the junior English course will meet in the media center's computer lab and each student will use the Internet to access the following sites: www.gcic.peachnet.edu and www.augustachronicle.com

Procedures:

As a behavior management strategy, students are given a red folded stock paper placard to be placed on their monitor when they have a question. As the students enter the media center, they draw a career card from the Careers Basket. Students are paired by seat assignments for the completion of their Budget Form and their group presentations. Students are given the following materials: Student Directions, Career Draw: Your First Job worksheet and the Budget Form. The students access the Internet sites and use the Student Directions as their guide for completing the assignments. During the last fifteen minutes of the class period, the students meet in their groups to share their findings and plan their class presentations. On the following day, students complete their individual assignments, meet in their groups, and make their group presentations to the class. The student materials are collected and evaluated according to the value of each question on the rubric.

Assessment:

Students may earn a total of 25 points for a quiz grade in their English class. The rubrics of the Budget Form and Career Draw: Your First Job are used to evaluate the performance of the students. The grades are recorded and given to the English teachers.

Materials/Technology Needed:

Red stock paper placards, Student Directions, Career Draw: Your First Job worksheet and Budget Form worksheet, computers in the media center and access to the Internet.

LESSON PLAN 2 WORKSHEET 2A

Career Draw: Your First Job

Student Directions:

1. Draw a Career Card from the Careers Basket.

2. Write your initials and Career Title by your name on the Class Roster.

3. Go to www.gcic.peachnet.edu

4. Put cursor on Run GCIS. Put in the identification and password.

5. Under the occupations list, find your Career and answer the following questions using paragraphs and complete sentences:
   - What is the nature of the work? Give information from the Overview and Work Activities.
   - What are three work aptitudes needed for this career?
   - What is the work setting? Give a description of where you would work.
   - What is the Georgia average wage per month and per year?
   - How many workers were employed in this career in Augusta in 2000 and how many are projected for 2006? Is the number of workers increasing or decreasing?
   - What are four of the tools that may be used in this job?
   - What is the preparation needed to get this job?

6. Complete the Budget Form. Enter the Career and the amount of monthly salary and annual salary.

7. Go to www.augustachronicle.com. Access information about apartment or mobile home rentals.

8. Pair with your computer partner to share living expenses in planning your budget.

9. Form a small group of four to present your findings to the class.

LESSON PLAN 2 WORKSHEET 2B

Budget Form

Name: _____   Date: _____

Monthly Salary: _____

Housing	Rent or Mortgage Electricity/Gas Water Telephone Garbage Service Cleaning, maintenance, repairs	$_____ $_____ $_____ $_____ $_____ $_____ Total $_____
Food	Supermarket/Grocery Store Eating Out	$_____ $_____ Total $_____
Clothing	Purchase of New Clothes Dry Cleaning, Laundry	$_____ $_____ Total $_____
Transportation	Car/Truck Payments Gas Maintenance, repairs Public Transportation (bus, subway, taxi)	$_____ $_____ $_____ $_____ Total $_____
Bills and Debts	Credit Cards Loans	$_____ $_____ Total $_____
Taxes	Federal—Income & Social Security State Local/property Tax help (accountant)	$_____ $_____ $_____ $_____ Total $_____
Insurance	Car Medical or health care House and possessions Life	$_____ $_____ $_____ $_____ Total $_____
Medical Expenses	Doctor Dentist Prescriptions Fitness	$_____ $_____ $_____ $_____ Total $_____
Amusement	Movies, Concerts, Shows, Other	Total $_____

LESSON PLAN THREE

Title: Preparing for the PSAT

Objectives:

- To identify the reasons for taking the Preliminary SAT/National Merit Scholarship Qualifying Test.
- To identify the parts of the PSAT and to describe the kinds of questions in each section.
- To practice for the college entrance examinations by taking a practice test online.

Technology Connection: Internet

Procedures:

1. The school counselor introduces the lesson by asking the students to respond to the question "What does it take to get into a college?"

2. Students are given a "Preparing for the PSAT" worksheet.

3. Students discuss achievement including the grade point average and college entrance exams.

4. Students discuss reasons for taking the PSAT.

5. The school counselor will give an overview of the PSAT/NMSQT.

6. Students will access the following Web site: www.collegeboard.com

7. On the homepage, the students will go to the PSAT introductory page by clicking the cursor on PSAT/NMSQT under the college board test button.

8. The students will answer the sample questions in each section of the PSAT.

9. Upon completion of the sample items, the students will complete the worksheet.

10. The lesson will conclude with a class discussion of the items on the worksheet.

Materials and Technology Needed:

- Internet
- Worksheet
- PSAT Student Bulletins

Special Note: This lesson may be modified to use the ACT's PLAN Assessment.

Related URL: www.act.org/plan/

LESSON PLAN 3 WORKSHEET

Preparing for the PSAT: Student Guide to Preparation

1. Since the best preparation for college and the PSAT is long term, what are the main ingredients in this recipe for successful planning?

2. Prior to the test, what are five actions that the student should do to be ready for the PSAT?

3. What are the three parts of the PSAT?

4. List and describe the kinds of questions in the Verbal section of the test.

5. List and describe the kinds of questions in the Math section of the test.

6. The Writing Skills section of the PSAT has questions about the following kinds of skills: identifying sentence errors, improving sentences, and improving paragraphs. What is the purpose of each of these sections in measuring skills related to editing and revising?

7. List five "I learned" statements from the experience of answering the sample test items.

LESSON PLAN FOUR

Title: Picture Me—My Self-Portrait

Lesson Objectives:

- Students will identify personal characteristics, interests, and abilities.
- Students will identify which personal characteristics are needed for employment.

Technology Connections:

The eighth-grade English class will use digital cameras to take photographs of each student and then each student will use the computer/printer to print a picture with a description.

Procedures:

To help develop a positive self-concept, discuss how each student is unique, different, and special. Begin with a discussion of physical differences and ask each student to list a physical characteristic. To help with the physical description, students will work in triads to take digital pictures and save and print the pictures. Under the picture, the students print a description of themselves. When the students have finished this activity, the groups of three now identify a positive character trait of each member. After the small group sharing, allow volunteers to share their personal characteristics with the class. As the students report their findings, ask the class if others share that same trait. Discuss how each student has personal traits that can help them have a happy, successful life and rewarding career. Distribute the activity sheet "Self-Portrait in Words" and give the students time to complete it. Upon completion of the activity sheet, have students return to the triad and share what they have learned about their personal characteristics, interests, and abilities. Allow volunteers to share their findings. Ask the class what personal traits are important in getting and keeping a job.

Brainstorm ways to improve or develop positive traits. Conclude the lesson by emphasizing the connection between personal characteristics and skills needed in the workplace.

Assessment:

Large and small group participation, completion of digital photo, and "Self-Portrait in Words" activity sheet.

Materials/Technology Needed:

Digital cameras, computers, printers, and "Self-Portrait in Words" activity sheet.

LESSON PLAN 4 WORKSHEET

Self-Portrait in Words

Everyone has positive and negative personal traits. The positive ones are desirable and helpful in getting and keeping a job. As you identify your personal characteristics, interests, and abilities, you will become more aware of yourself and how you can develop more desirable qualities that will help you get the job that you want.

Circle the personal characteristic, interests, and abilities that best describe you. Be honest. If you have others that are not listed, write them under "others."

PERSONAL CHARACTERISTICS

Initiative	Critical	Assertive	Respectful	Polite
Industrious	Sloppy	Careless	Flexible	Unorganized
Responsible	Disrespectful	Unmotivated	Competitive	Tardy
Punctual	Neat	Flexible	Versatile	Attentive
Trustworthy	Aggressive	Talkative	Lazy	*Others*
Loyal	Irresponsible	Articulate	Sensitive	
Cheerful	Friendly	Organized	Careful	
Moody	Intelligent	Motivated	Resourceful	

INTERESTS

Outdoor	Computational	Persuasive	Literary	Social Service
Mechanical	Scientific	Artistic	Musical	Clerical
Investigative	Computer	Medicine	Entertainment	*Others*
Public Service	Technology	Health	Sports	

ABILITIES AND SKILLS

Mechanical	Scientific	Artistic	Teaching	Computer
Constructing	Organizing	Musical	Writing	Skills
Repairing	Planning	Entertaining	Selling	Cooking
Measuring	Researching	Acting	Reading	Serving
Assembling	Problem Solving	Drawing	Driving	*Others*

From the circled words above, select the 10 that describe you the best:

1. _____ 2. _____ 3. _____ 4. _____ 5. _____

6. _____ 7. _____ 8. _____ 9. _____ 10. _____

From your circled words of Personal Characteristics, list six that employers want in an employee:

1. _____ 2. _____ 3. _____

4. _____ 5. _____ 6. _____

LESSON PLAN 5

Title: My Personal Goals

Lesson Objectives:

- To recognize the difference between goals and daydreams.
- To identify the elements of a clearly defined goal.
- To prepare a Power Point presentation illustrating five long-range lifetime goals.

Technology Connections:

The ninth-grade Social Studies class will meet in the computer lab to prepare a PowerPoint presentation illustrating five long-range lifetime goals.

Procedures:

Introduce the lesson by giving each student a sheet of paper, which will be folded in half vertically and then horizontally, forming four rectangle sections or windows. After the students open the folded paper, it is placed in the landscape view (horizontal) and the following directions are given: In the top left window, list something that you want to accomplish this week. In the top right window, write something that you want to do by the end of the semester. In the bottom left window, list a goal that you want to reach within the next four years. In the bottom right window, write a goal that you want to accomplish by the end of ten years. Allow volunteers to share their personal goals with the class. Ask the class to identify the two types of goals that were presented in the introductory activity. Short-range goals are activities that can be accomplished now or within three or four months. Long-range goals involve a greater amount time for attainment. Discuss with the class the difference between a goal and a daydream. Usually daydreams are something that we wish to attain, but we do not make a specific action plan to reach our dream. Discuss the following elements of a reachable goal:

- Specific and Clear
- Personal
- Measurable
- Challenging
- Realistic
- Written with time limits

After the discussion, distribute the activity sheet "My Personal Goals," and allow students time to complete it. As the students work on the activity, circulate around the room to check progress and answer questions. Following the activity, let students share their goals with the class. Explain that students will use the activity sheets in the development of the PowerPoint presentation. The students will complete the slides for their presentation in the computer lab and present their findings to the class.

Assessment:

Participation in the class discussion, completion of "My Personal Goals" activity sheet, and the PowerPoint presentation.

Materials/Technology:

"My Personal Goals" activity sheet, PowerPoint software, and computers in computer lab.

LESSON PLAN 5 WORKSHEET

My Personal Goals

Part A. Elements of an Attainable Goal

Fill in the blanks.

1. _____: describes what you want to accomplish with as much detail as possible and is stated so that anyone can understand what you want to do.

2. _____: the goals relate to you and what you want to accomplish.

3. _____: describes your goal in terms that can be evaluated so that you know when you have reached your goal.

4. _____: takes energy and discipline to accomplish and involves managing a plan to accomplish the goal.

5. _____: you know that you are capable of obtaining the goal.

6. _____: the goal is put in writing and you set a realistic date or point in time to achieve it. This may involve breaking a long-range goal into short-range goals with specific target completion dates.

Part B. Planning My Life Goals

Answer the following questions about yourself without a great deal of thought.

• What do you want to accomplish in life?

_____

_____

• Do you feel capable or in charge of making things happen in your life?

_____

_____

Part C. Setting My Life-Style Goals

If you want something to happen in your life, you must make a place for it to happen. Setting goals can help you to do this by giving you control in your life rather than allowing events and situations to merely happen to you. Begin by stating a goal related to the job that you really want to have. Remember to follow the elements of an attainable goal.

1. My Career Goal:

_____

_____

2. My Education Goal:

_____

_____

3. My Social Goal: (single, married, family)

_____

_____

4. My Living Environment: (home, style, location)

_____

_____

5. My Work Environment: (inside, outside, location)

_____

_____

6. My Leisure Activities:

_____

_____

RESOURCE 3.9

Recommended Career Center References and Resources

Web Sites:

- See Chapter 5 for Suggested Links (e.g., Career, College, Homework)

Books:

- *100 Best Careers for the 21st Century*
- *Barron's 300 Best Buys for a College Education*
- *Barron's Profiles of American Colleges*
- *Career Choices: A Guide for Teens and Young Adults*
- *Career Guide to Industries*
- *Careersmarts: Jobs With a Future*
- *College Costs and Financial Aid Handbook 2003*
- *Complete Guide for Occupational Exploration*
- *Electronic Résumé Revolution: Creating a Winning Résumé for the New World of Job Seeking*
- *Exploring Tech Careers: Real People Tell You What You Need to Know*
- *Free and Inexpensive Career Materials: A Resource Directory*
- *Helping Your Child Choose a Career*
- *High Impact Résumés and Letters*
- *Index of Majors and Graduate Degrees 2003*
- *Military Careers*
- *Occupational Outlook Handbook*
- *Peterson's Vocational and Technical Schools and Programs*
- *Peterson's Four-Year Colleges 2003*
- *Peterson's Two-Year Colleges 2003*
- *Personal and Career Exploration*
- *Succeeding in the World of Work*
- *The American Almanac of Jobs and Salaries*
- *The Dictionary of Occupational Titles*
- *The Enhanced Occupational Outlook Handbook*
- *The Occupational Outlook Quarterly*
- *What Color Is Your Parachute?*

Newsletters/Publications

- Career Opportunities News
- Spotlight
- The Job Hunting Handbook: Job Outlook to 2005

Publishers

- ACT Career Planning Services
- American Guidance Services

- Career Communications, Inc.
- Chronicle Guidance Publications
- Enter Here L.L.C
- Fearon/Janus Education
- Ferguson Publishing Company
- Impact Publication
- Kaplan Books
- Lakeshore Learning Materials
- Peterson's Guides
- Psychological Assessment Resources, Inc.
- Sunburst Communications, Inc.
- Walch J. Weston Publisher

FORM 3.1

Career Development Plan

Directions: The career development plan form assists the school counselor to plan a comprehensive career development program by grade level. Select a career development area, competencies, and performance indicators to support the target area. Note all activities that will demonstrate mastery of the concept. In addition, note all materials and resources necessary to conduct the activities.

Grade: _____   School Year: _____

AREA OF CAREER DEVELOPMENT: _____

(Self-Knowledge, Educational and Occupational Exploration, and Career Planning)

COMPETENCY: _____

PERFORMANCE INDICATORS:

1. _____

2. _____

3. _____

4. _____

5. _____

STUDENT ACTIVITIES:

1. _____

2. _____

3. _____

4. _____

5. _____

REQUIRED MATERIALS OR RESOURCES:

_____

_____

_____

_____

FORM 3.2

Job Shadowing Application

STUDENT NAME: _____

             FIRST   MIDDLE   LAST

CURRENT GRADE: _____

DOB: _____ SS# _____

MAILING ADDRESS: _____

_____

_____

HOME TELEPHONE: _____

FATHER'S NAME: _____

WORKPLACE: _____

WORK TELEPHONE: _____

MOTHER'S NAME: _____

WORKPLACE: _____

WORK TELEPHONE: _____

EDUCATION GOAL: _____

_____

CAREER GOAL: _____

_____

CAREER AREA OR JOB SITE THAT YOU WOULD LIKE TO VISIT FOR A DAY AS A JOB SHADOWING EXPERIENCE:

_____

_____

FORM 3.3

Internship Application

STUDENT INFORMATION

STUDENT NAME: _____

| FIRST | MIDDLE | LAST |

Current Grade: _____

DOB: _____   SS# _____

MAILING ADDRESS: _____

_____

_____

HOME TELEPHONE: _____

CAREER AREA OF INTEREST: _____

INTERNSHIP LOCATION: _____

INTERNSHIP SUPERVISOR: _____

PLEASE EXPLAIN WHY YOU ARE REQUESTING AN INTERNSHIP POSITION:

_____

_____

_____

_____

PARENT INFORMATION: _____

PARENT OR GUARDIAN NAME: _____

WORKPLACE: _____

WORK TELEPHONE: _____

Best Practice 4

Create Transition Programs That Prepare Students for Success

Best Practice 4: Create Transition Programs That Prepare Students for Success

Counselors must develop programs that assist, facilitate, and promote the smooth transition of middle and high school students to the next level of education or direct entry into the modern workforce. Students need assistance with setting goals, developing study and time management skills, achieving in high-level academic courses, and obtaining the academic skills necessary to become independent learners. In this chapter, we present three transition programs that focus on academic skill remediation, study skills, extra help, and postsecondary exploration and planning. The transition programs are grade specific and designed to support students when entering the ninth grade and throughout the high school experience. Students need a strong academic foundation and continuous support as they prepare for new educational and work experiences. This chapter provides step-by-step guides for developing and implementing three programs that will assist students to transition from eighth to ninth grade, progress from ninth through twelfth grade, and transition to postsecondary endeavors. Goals, objectives, forms, and organizational steps are included for each program.

SECTION 1: A KEYSTONE PROGRAM FOR RISING NINTH-GRADE STUDENTS

The keystone is the vital stone that holds everything in place, and the Keystone Program gives ninth graders a purpose and vision for the high school experience. It also supports the transition from middle school to high school. In today's fast-paced, complicated society, students have the following concerns about moving from middle school to high school:

- Being tardy to class (getting to class on time), finding lockers, navigating crowded hallways, and getting lost
- Being victimized or harassed by others
- Being safe at school
- Being able to understand difficult classes
- Coping with rigid rules and strict teachers
- Being able to make new friends in a new setting (Queen, 2002, p. 21)

The school counselor works with the ninth-grade faculty to develop and implement activities that will facilitate the transition from middle to high school. As the students progress through their programs of study and various courses, they will begin to see how the experiences of the ninth grade have enabled them to arrive in the twelfth grade ready to demonstrate their skills and abilities in the Capstone Program of their senior year. It truly becomes their crowning achievement, and the seeds for this abundant harvest are sown in the ninth-grade year.

Goals of the Keystone Program

The major goal of the Keystone is to assist ninth graders to understand the high school programs of study in relation to their personal and career goals. In addition, the activities of the program help ninth graders make a smooth transition to high school. The students are introduced to the various programs and career pathways that the high school offers. Through the various activities, the ninth-graders learn about themselves and continue to answer the question "Who am I?" In addition, the students learn how to communicate with their peers and adults while acquiring information about life skills and careers.

Steps to Organizing the Keystone Program

1. Establish the Keystone Program Committee. The committee is composed of teachers of the ninth-grade core areas, career technical education teachers, school counselors, and administrators. The committee meets monthly to plan the rising ninth graders' transition program and to monitor the current ninth-grade project.

2. The committee meets in September to set the theme, objectives, and activities for the rising ninth grade's Keystone Program.

3. The committee develops a timeline for the ninth-grade project and places the dates on the school's calendar.

4. The committee develops and updates the teacher's handbook and student's handbook for the program.

5. The committee develops and reviews the list of resources and materials needed to implement the program.

6. The committee plans and conducts a staff development program to train the teachers in implementing the Keystone Program.

7. In parent and student orientation programs, the school counselors explain the components of the Keystone Program.

8. In the rising ninth-grade individual advisory meeting, the adviser explains to the parents and student the high school programs, the ninth-grade courses, and the Keystone Program.

9. The program is launched during the second week of school and is concluded the week before semester exams.

10. The committee conducts an evaluation of the program by surveying teachers, parents, and students.

Key Components

1. Ninth graders take the following courses: English, Algebra I, Introduction to Physics, Civics and Economics, Personal Fitness and Health, Computer Applications, and Keystone career course. The career course is the centerpiece of the Keystone Program. The main activities are coordinated through this course and the Keystone project is worth twenty-five percent of the Keystone career course's final grade.

2. To assist the new ninth graders in the transition to high school, the following activities are held during the first two weeks of the semester:

- For the first three days of school, homeroom teachers spend forty minutes each morning discussing the student handbook.
- The ninth graders are divided into two large groups for an orientation session with the school principal and counselors. The educators discuss the following issues: school safety, harassment and bullying, class schedules, important dates, study skills and note taking, semester exams, graduation requirements, and tips for surviving the first year of high school.
- The Keystone career teacher assists students to adjust to the new building by arranging orientation tours to the media center, school counseling office, Career Center, career technical classes, fine arts classes, and the core area departments. Throughout the semester, teams of students from the Keystone career class spend a period in one of the career technical classes and fine arts classes, so by the end of the semester the students have had the opportunity to explore each elective class.

3. Students are given a career interest inventory during the second week of school. The results of this instrument are matched to occupations. The student will select one career of interest and prepare a research paper. The ninth-grade English teachers will assist their classes to prepare the research papers. The Algebra I teachers will help students to develop graphs to illustrate the career data from their research and also help students prepare budgets based on the starting salary in their chosen career. The science department will teach problem-solving methods. The computer applications classes will assist the students to produce the research paper.

4. The students must have four sources of information for their papers and one of those sources must be an interview with a worker in their chosen career or one closely related. The interview may be via the phone or in person and must be recorded. In the Keystone career classes, the students give oral reports about their interview. In their English classes, the students will give oral reports about their research papers.

5. As part of the career research, students must describe the education and training required for their selected job. To connect school to the world of work, the Keystone career teacher introduces the career technical programs that are available in the high school and arranges inschool field trips to those classes and labs. In addition, the college preparatory programs are highlighted, and the requirements for college are discussed. To reinforce the school-to-work concept, the area Youth Apprenticeship Coordinator is invited to speak to all of the Keystone career classes.

6. During the last week of the semester before the exams, the Keystone career class is the scene of the Career Celebration. Students are dressed in the uniform or attire of their chosen career and skits are presented about the different careers. The research reports and graphs are displayed. Parents are encouraged to attend this concluding celebration activity.

SECTION 2: A CREDIT RECOVERY PROGRAM FOR HIGH SCHOOL STUDENTS

The high school curriculum is constantly increasing in substance and rigor in order to prepare students for the next level of education. Often, students need more time to learn course objectives and demonstrate mastery of skills than is permitted during a school term. Failure could affect a student's graduation status and hinder his or her progression from grade level to grade level. In addition, some high school courses have specific prerequisites, and students may miss taking a particular series if they do not pass the initial course (Math is a prime example). We have devised a credit recovery program (Project: HOPE) for students in grades nine through twelve that extends the school day and provides opportunities for students to regain credit. The program targets a specific group of students who have demonstrated some knowledge of a course area, but who need additional time to master all objectives.

Program Description

Project: HOPE is a credit recovery program offered to high school students who have failed a semester of a core class with a 62–69% average. The program meets for seven weeks in two-hour sessions four days a week. The primary focus is to extend the school day in order to provide students with extra time and opportunities to master important skills in core subject areas. All Project: HOPE teachers use Mastery Learning with a reteach/retest format. Teachers individually review identified deficit skills with all students and reteach/retest each skill area in order to ensure student mastery of the designated material. Students who successfully demonstrate mastery of identified course objectives at a predetermined level will be awarded credit at the conclusion of the session.

Program Goals

- To promote student mastery of academic skills in core subject areas.
- To provide students with opportunities for academic skill remediation, reinforcement, and enrichment.
- To assist students in their efforts to meet all state graduation requirements and to stay on track for high school graduation.

Student Eligibility

- Students must be currently enrolled and in good standing at their home school.
- Students must have failed a core class with a 62%–69% average.
- Students must have been absent fewer than ten days during the semester.
- Students must have received no discipline referrals for inappropriate behavior in the core class they failed.
- Students must have a referral from the core area teacher documenting their skill deficits.
- Students must have written parent permission to participate in Project: HOPE.
- Students must have written permission to ride the bus provided for program participants.

Instructional Staff

- All Project: HOPE teachers are certified in their assigned subject areas.

Teacher Guidelines

- Project: HOPE teachers will use Mastery Learning as the primary instructional approach throughout the program.
- How to instruct for mastery:

  1. Major objectives representing the purposes of the course or unit define mastery of the subject.

  2. The subject is divided into relatively small learning units, each with its own objectives and assessment.

  3. Learning materials and instructional strategies are identified. Teaching, modeling, practice, formative evaluation, reteaching and reinforcement, and summative evaluation are included.

  4. Each unit is preceded by brief diagnostic tests.

5. The results of diagnostic tests are used to provide supplementary instruction to help students overcome problems.

6. No student is to proceed to new material until basic prerequisite material is mastered.

- Project: HOPE teachers must obtain all needed materials from their department heads.
- Project: HOPE teachers will be given a class roster, which will list the name of each student and his or her identified deficit areas.
- Project: HOPE teachers will individually review deficit skill areas with each student the first day of class.
- Project: HOPE teachers must keep a daily attendance record. Students must be dropped from the program after three absences.
- Project: HOPE teachers must contact parents of students who are not making progress in the program.
- Project: HOPE teachers must issue a final report card to each student at the completion of the program.
- Project: HOPE classes will not meet on teacher staff development or parent conference dates.

The following forms are found in this section:

Form 4.1 Project: HOPE Student Referral

SECTION 3: A CAPSTONE PROGRAM FOR TWELFTH-GRADE STUDENTS

Leading educators, government leaders, business executives, and education reform groups are calling for a "meaningful senior year in high school" (SREB, 2002, p. 5). "A senior project provides an opportunity for a student to choose an area of interest, conduct in-depth research, and demonstrate problem-solving, decision-making and independent living skills" (Murray, 2002, p. 19). The effective school counselor teams with administrators and teachers to design and implement a senior year Capstone Program that will help students prepare for their next step. The Capstone Program represents the high point in a student's achievement in high school. Seniors use the knowledge, skills, and information gained from their previous years of learning to plan, implement, and present a comprehensive project involving problem solving, research, synthesis or product development, and oral presentations of their findings to a board of teachers and community representatives. The program also involves the development of an action plan for postsecondary education and employment. Although the Capstone Program is so instructionally intensive that a teacher may have two periods a day to coordinate the project, the school counselor remains a key player in assisting seniors in the transition from high school to postsecondary educational and career opportunities.

Goals of the Capstone Program

The major goal of the Capstone Program is to allow seniors to engage in meaningful learning experiences and "stretch" their intellectual development by developing a research paper, a product or service portfolio, and an oral presentation. The students will learn to problem solve, plan, develop schedules, and work with the school staff, community members, and business leaders to complete their senior project. The twelfth graders will develop a plan of action for the next step after high school.

Steps to Organizing the Capstone Program

1. Establish the Capstone Program Committee. The committee is composed of the senior project coordinator, representative teachers from the academic core and career technical areas, school counselors, media specialist, Career Center specialist, and administrator.

2. The committee meets in October to set the objectives and activities for the rising senior class's Capstone Program.

3. The committee develops a timeline for the twelfth-grade project and places the dates on the school's calendar.

4. The committee develops and updates the teacher's handbook and student's handbook for the next year.

5. The committee develops and updates the list of resources and materials needed to implement the program.

6. The committee plans and conducts a staff development program to train the teachers to implement the components of the Capstone Program.

7. During the final session of the schoolwide advisement program, the junior advisers will preview the key parts of the Capstone Program with their rising seniors.

8. In parent and student orientation programs, the senior project coordinator and the school counselors explain the essential elements of the senior project.

9. The program is launched during the second week of school as the English teachers distribute the Capstone Program Student Manuals and explain the specific requirements of the program.

10. During the first ten days of school, each senior selects a faculty member as adviser for the project. A faculty member may only have five or fewer students to assist.

11. The program concludes in April during College and Career Day.

12. The committee conducts an evaluation of the program by surveying teachers, parents, and students.

Key Components

1. Since all seniors are required to take the fourth year of English, it is the centerpiece of the Capstone Program. The main activities are coordinated through this course, and the senior project is worth twenty-five percent of the English IV grade. In addition, the school counselors and the Career Center specialist assist each senior to develop a post-high school plan of action.

2. During the second week of the first semester, English teachers distribute and highlight the main sections of the Capstone Program Student Manual. The main sections of the handbook include
   - General information: timelines, policies, and grading procedures
   - Topic selection: interest inventory, project proposals, and parent forms
   - Role of the mentor and faculty adviser: mentor forms and adviser logs
   - Preliminary work: letter and signature of intent, interview, annotated bibliography, and rubrics
   - Research paper: sources, note cards, thesis statement, outline, format, and rubric
   - Product development: planning sheet, contract, verification log, and rubric
   - Portfolio development: items checklist, sample letter to judges, and rubric
   - Preparation for the school/community boards: guidelines, visual and audio aids, delivery and appearance, planning sheet, and rubric

3. During the first month of school, each senior meets with the school counselor and the Career Center specialist to develop a post-high school plan of action that includes
   a. educational and career goals
   b. steps needed to reach goal
   c. education or training options (technical colleges, four-year colleges, universities, apprenticeship programs, armed services, and specialized training)
   d. admissions tests (e.g., ACT, ASSET, SAT, and ASVAB)
   e. financial aid and scholarship planning
   f. part-time work while a student
   g. student housing, if applicable

Upon completion of the plan, the school counselor meets with the student and reviews the plan. After review, the action plan is placed in the student's Capstone Program Portfolio.

4. The preliminary parts of the project—including the research proposal, letter of intent, interview with expert or mentor, and annotated bibliography—are due the last week of the first term.

5. The research paper is due the fifth week of the second term. The note cards, outline, and first draft of the research paper are due the third and fourth weeks of the second term. This work represents twenty-five percent of the second term's grade.

6. The students complete the product during the third term, and present the demonstrations or findings to their English class by the third week of February.

7. Periodically during the year, the student's Capstone Program Portfolio is reviewed by the English teachers. During the last week of February, all faculty members are given several portfolios to evaluate using the portfolio rubric. After evaluation, each portfolio is returned to the appropriate English teacher so the student's grade may be recorded. The portfolio and the product presentation to the English classes are worth twenty-five percent of the student's third term grade.

8. The final element in the Capstone Project is the board presentation. The board is composed of three community representatives and two faculty members. The student is given ten minutes to present the research, product, career plans, and evaluation of the project. Another five minutes are given for questions and answers. The board members use the product presentation rubric to assign grades. Following the presentation, the rubrics are collected and sent to a central location in the school where the judges tally each student's scores, dropping the highest and lowest scores and keeping the middle scores to assign the student's grade. This grade is worth twenty-five percent of the student's fourth term grade in English.

The following forms are found in this section:

Form 4.2 Capstone Post-High School Plan of Action Worksheet

FORM 4.1

Project: HOPE Student Referral

Student Name: _____   Date:_____

Referring Teacher: _____

Failed Course Name and Course Number: _____

School Year and Semester: _____

Final Course Grade	Deficit Skill Area (Specific Chapters and/or Concepts)

Referring Teacher Comments:

_____

_____

_____

_____

_____

_____

_____

FORM 4.2

Capstone Post-High School Plan of Action Worksheet

1. Education Goals:

2. Steps Needed to Reach Goals:

3. Career Goals:

4. Steps Needed to Reach Goals:

5. Education and Training Options (Technical College, Two-Year and/or Four-Year College or University):

6. Apprenticeship Programs, Armed Services, and Specialized Training:

7. Financial Aid/Scholarship Planning:

8. Part-Time Employment While a Student:

9. Student Housing, if Applicable:

Best Practice 5

Establish and Maintain Communication With the School Community

Best Practice 5: Establish and Maintain Communication With the School Community

School faculty and staff must establish and maintain an effective communication system in order to build solid partnerships with all stakeholders. According to Riley (in Moles, 1996), "it is well known that when families, educators, and communities all work together, schools get better and students get the high quality education they need to lead productive lives" (p. iii). According to Berger (1995), "one-way communication informs parents about the school's plans and happenings. Two-way communication allows parents to feed into the school their knowledge, concerns, and desires and requires interaction between the participants" (p. 162). The school counselor plays a critical role in devising a system that includes both forms of communication. Typically, a school's counseling staff is responsible for informing stakeholders about academic programs, services, and resources (one-way communication); conducting parent-teacher conferences, orientation sessions, and workshops; and formulating parent groups to address specific issues or concerns (two-way communication). A school counselor is a trained communicator and must use his or her skills to assist teachers and administrators in their efforts to positively connect with families. "Communication, both nonverbal and verbal, is the 'stuff' that initiates, builds, maintains, and destroys relationships" (Miller, Wackman, Nunnally, & Miller, 1988, p. 9).

This chapter provides effective strategies for establishing and maintaining a two-way communication system with the school community. The strategies are designed to build trust and rapport with parents and provide parents with "opportunities to exchange information and support, which parents find to be more rewarding and empowering than simply being the recipients of educator's expertise" (Swap, 1993, p. 159). The strategies revolve around conducting successful and productive parent conferences; conducting informative parent orientations and workshops; and developing creative and user-friendly Web pages as a means to reach all stakeholders. We have included forms and resources that will be useful to school counselors, faculty, and staff.

SECTION 1: ESTABLISHING COMMUNICATION

Strategy 1: Parent Conferences

A parent conference is an excellent two-way communication strategy to build rapport and trust with parents. School counselors conduct numerous parent conferences during the school year and organize and facilitate many more involving teachers, administrators, and other support personnel. Minke and Anderson (2003) found two primary themes to be supported in traditional parent conferences:

> (1) parents and teachers agreed that conferences are important opportunities for information exchange, with the major purpose of teachers giving information to parents; and (2) parents and teachers approach conferences with varying degrees of trepidation. (p. 57)

A parent conference tends to be a more personable and productive method of communicating with parents and provides less chance for the misinterpretation of information, as compared to the one-way communication of progress reports and newsletters. The school counselor should assist faculty and staff to develop and perfect their conferencing skills by focusing on positive speaking, rephrasing, and attentive listening. Berger (1995) provides teachers with the following twelve qualities of good communicators:

1. Give their total attention to the speaker.
2. Restate the parents' concerns.
3. Show respect for the other person.
4. Recognize the parents' feelings.
5. Tailor discussions to fit the parents' ability to handle the situation.
6. Do not touch off the fuse of a parent who might not be able to handle a child's difficulties.
7. Emphasize that concerns are no one's fault.
8. Remember that no one ever wins an argument.

9. Protect the parents' egos.

10. Focus on one issue at a time.

11. Listen.

12. Become allies with parents. (p. 276)

Parents need to leave each conference feeling that someone truly understands their concerns and confident that any plans or strategies developed during the conference will be implemented and monitored by school officials. Unfortunately, conferences are not always pleasant experiences for school officials or parents. Faculty and staff need guidelines for dealing with angry parents. We found the list of suggestions created by Morehead (2001) to be beneficial for counselors, teachers, and parents (see Resource 5.1). Also, we have created a checklist for parents to help maximize the benefits of a school conference (see Resource 5.2). A parent conference requires a tremendous amount of planning by the school counselor. The two most common types of parent conferences are the academic progress conference and the problem-solving conference. We have provided a checklist for each type of conference to assist the school counselor in his or her conference preparation and ensure a successful and productive meeting.

The following forms are found in this section:

Form 5.1 Conducting a Successful Parent Conference

Form 5.2 Conference Minutes

Strategy 2: Parent and Student Orientation Sessions

The effective school counselor must be adept at organizing and conducting orientation sessions. Typically, one of the major responsibilities of a school's counseling staff is the coordination of program activities, events, and resources. The school counselor serves three major populations in preparing for group guidance programs: students, faculty and administrators, and parents (Morganett, 1990). Implementing orientation programs requires thorough planning. The planning process assists the counselor to stay focused as he or she prepares informative sessions for students, parents, and teachers. A word of caution: it is best to start simply and then expand on the things that work. The following planning formula is adapted from Morganett's work.

Step 1: Form a Committee

The size of the committee is a function of the magnitude of the orientation project (schoolwide, grade, department, or specific group). For example, the number of committee members for the advanced placement orientation program is fewer than for the rising ninth-grade parents and students orientation. The committee ought to include students, parents, faculty, and administrators. The school counselor's training and work responsibilities are assets to the leadership of the committee. The committee will complete the major tasks of planning, implementing, and evaluating the orientation program.

Step 2: Conduct a Needs Assessment

As noted earlier, the school counselor serves the three major populations of the school: students, faculty and administrators, and parents. Each of these groups is a source of information regarding the services needed, problem areas that need attention, and other topics that need to be addressed in the meetings. A specific needs assessment can be conducted to determine the topics to be included in the sessions. Different survey forms are developed for each group—students, parents, and teachers. The results are used to prepare agendas, to select topics, to select program speakers, and to determine the length of the orientation sessions.

Step 3: Develop a Written Plan

After the data from the needs assessment have been reviewed, the committee is able to develop a plan of action. The purpose of the program is developed as well as the description, goals, and objectives of the activity. Next, the logistics of the orientation sessions are developed. These include the "who, what, when, and how" of the program. The following questions are helpful when formulating the plan:

- Who will participate in the sessions, and who will lead the program?
- When and where will the orientation be held?
- How will the publicity be implemented?
- What are the evaluation procedures?
- What is the main content of the program and what materials and activities are necessary?
- What is the timeline for the various steps of the program preparation including the planning, implementation, and evaluation?

Step 4: Promote the Orientation Program

Once the plans and timeline have been completed, the program must be advertised. Notices of the orientation may be sent to local radio and television stations to be aired during the public service announcements. In addition, newspaper interviews are an excellent way to inform the public of the event; often the education reporter is looking for interesting information about local schools. One of the best means to let parents and students know about the activity is to send a letter home, and post the information on the school counselor's Web page.

Step 5: Conduct the Event

Arrange to have a welcoming committee ready at least thirty minutes before the start of the program. Students of one of the school's service clubs may serve as greeters to welcome, distribute agendas or other materials, and to give directions for seating. When the guest speakers and other program personalities arrive, the students will take them to the hospitality room for refreshments and to receive any last minute instructions. Begin the meeting on time and remind participants to complete the evaluation forms at the conclusion of the presentations. After the meeting, allow time for questions and comments. End the session on time, but remind the audience that the speakers will remain for a few minutes to answer individual questions and concerns.

Step 6: Conduct the Evaluation

The evaluations are collected and tabulated following the orientation event. The results are shared with the orientation committee and used to make appropriate modifications in the program. Also, the information must be used to determine if the presentations are making a difference in the achievement of students. To do this, the data must be kept several years so comparisons can be made to assess the impact of the program. For example, in the advanced placement program orientation, students and parents complete an evaluation form that will help the committee determine the effectiveness of the meeting. The data from the participants attending the event will be used to determine the number of students who actually took advanced placement exams and received scores high enough for college credit.

SECTION 2: MAINTAINING COMMUNICATION

Strategy 1: Parent Workshops

Parent workshops are beneficial to the school and community and provide the school's counseling staff with the opportunity to develop a bridge of understanding and communication with parents. The planning process for parent workshops is quite similar to that of the orientation events. The school counselor is a leader in the development of the parent workshops. These programs allow parents to learn new skills and practice existing skills. The following steps will help the school counseling team conduct quality parent workshops.

Step 1: The School Counseling Team Meets

Prior to the beginning of the school year, the school counseling team meets to develop the annual action plan and calendar. The members of the team include the counselors and the clerical staff. In some cases, the assistant principal for student learning/services may be included in the planning session. Roles and responsibilities are determined for each school counselor. An individual is designated as the leader of the parent workshop project. In large schools, it may be appropriate to have more than one counselor to serve in this capacity. During this initial meeting, a calendar of counseling events is developed including the tentative dates for the parent workshops.

Step 2: Develop a Needs Assessment

The school counselor designs a simple needs assessment survey to collect information from parents regarding topics of importance. The instrument ought to address specific issues and problems; however, target problems do not change significantly within a year or two. With that in mind, it may not be necessary to do a detailed parents' needs assessment every year, although the counselor will need to survey parents yearly to determine the major topics to be included in the parent workshops.

Step 3: Develop Action Plans

After reviewing the results of the needs assessment, the school counselor begins to formulate strategies for the implementation of the parent workshops. First, the main topics of interest are noted and given priority in the development of sessions. For example, if parents have indicated on previous surveys that financial aid information and career planning are the most important areas of concern, the counselor develops programs in those areas. In the action plan, the following ought to be considered: goals, objectives, logistics, and resources. The goals and objectives of the program are listed in an effort to keep the planning focused and to give direction to the process. The logistics include the "who, what, when, and where" of the workshop. The resources are the session leaders and the materials to be used in the presentations. While planning the workshops, the school counselor must consider how the program will be evaluated.

Step 4: Advertise the Workshop

The parents must be informed of the date, time, and location of the workshops. The local media will publicize school workshops as public service announcements. Usually the announcements must be sent to the news organizations a minimum of two weeks before the event. Sending letters to parents and posting the information of the school counselor's Web page are other ways to promote the event. One of best ways to inform parents of the activities is by a personal phone call. Forming a phone committee and spending a few hours calling parents will increase the attendance at the workshops.

Step 5: Conduct the Workshop

The school counselor makes arrangements for welcoming participants and resource speakers to the meeting. An icebreaker activity is an excellent way to begin the event. The counselor may be the facilitator of the session and introduce the presenters, or may be the primary presenter. For example, in the career planning workshop, the school counselor may be the program leader as he or she assists parents to identify interests, skills, and work values. The counselor may use the computer lab and the Internet to assist parents with career planning. In other situations, the counselor will introduce the presenters for the workshop, essentially serving as the master of ceremonies. For example, in a financial aid workshop, the presenters may be the state financial aid consultants and the financial aid representatives from the local colleges. After the presentation, a question and comment period will conclude the workshop.

Step 6: Evaluate the Workshop

The school counseling team needs to determine the most appropriate means of evaluating the workshop. Securing information from the participants is crucial to improve the quality of the parent workshops. The counselors must determine whether the program is meeting the goal and objectives stated in the action plan. The evaluation may consist of a pencil-and-paper instrument, a computer-assisted survey, or a pre/post measure of parents' degree of progress in learning the skills taught in the workshop.

Strategy 2: Create an Informative and User-Friendly Web Page

In the past several years, computer technology has become a powerful tool for facilitating communication. "Technology can assist in communicating a message which can be received at the convenience of the target audience without the barriers of space, place, or time" (Sabella & Booker, 2003, p. 207). An informative, user-friendly Web page and e-mail account will maximize the school counselor's ability to disseminate and receive information. We reviewed the Web sites of the top U.S. high schools identified by Matthews (2003), in an attempt to discover a standard format for a school counselor's or counseling department's Web site. We found that Web sites differ significantly in design, size, and type of information provided. In light of this discovery, we developed six categories of information for a school counselor's or counseling department's Web site. The reader is cautioned that Web sites are best when the design is simple and the site is updated regularly. Additionally, the counselor must remember that not every student and parent has access to the Internet, and critical information should continue to be distributed in hard copy. Resource 5.3 contains a number of Internet links that school counselors can use when constructing their Web pages.

Recommended Web Page Information

1. Meet Your School Counselor: School Counseling Department Personnel Information
   a. Staff pictures (use digital camera)
   b. Staff biographies
   c. Staff student assignments (e.g., alphabetical, grade level)
   d. Staff duties and areas of responsibility
   e. Staff telephone numbers and extensions
   f. Staff e-mail addresses

2. Counseling Department's Foundation
   a. Counselor beliefs
   b. Counseling department's mission statement
   c. Annual goals and objectives

3. Counseling Department's Policies and Procedures
   a. Hours of operation
   b. Annual student advisement sessions
   c. Annual registration procedures
   d. New student registration procedures
   e. Withdrawal procedures
   f. Graduation requirements
   g. Promotion criteria
   h. Retention criteria
   i. Academic eligibility criteria to participate in extracurricular activities
   j. Requesting transcripts
      i. Current students
      ii. Past graduates

   k. Requesting a counselor recommendation
   l. Requesting a conference with a school counselor
   m. Requesting a conference with a teacher

4. Parent and student information and resources
   a. Specific grade-level information
   b. School's course description catalog
   c. Six-year program planning guides for all programs of study and areas of concentration
   d. Monthly counseling department bulletin (noting important dates and upcoming events; specific college, career, and grade-level information; character word of the month; and other tidbits)
   e. Scholarship bulletin
   f. Web site links
      i. Colleges
      ii. Financial aid and scholarships
      iii. Careers
      iv. Career information for specific fields
      v. Homework help
      vi. College entrance exams
      vii. Selective service registration

5. General School Information
   a. Academic programs
      i. Advanced placement
      ii. Gifted and talented
      iii. Honors
      iv. International baccalaureate
      v. Special education

   b. School profile
   c. Special programs (e.g., schoolwide advisement, night school, online classes, tutoring services, SAT or ACT preparatory classes)
   d. Testing program and test dates (list point of contact)

ESTABLISH AND MAINTAIN COMMUNICATION

6. Frequently Used Forms
   a. School registration form
   b. Counselor recommendation form
   c. Teacher comments for recommendation form
   d. Parent information form
   e. Transcript request form
   f. College visitation request form
   g. Six-year program planning form

The following forms are found in this section:

Resource 5.1 Dealing With the Anger of Parents

Resource 5.2 Parent Tips for Conference Preparation

Resource 5.3 Web Sites for the School Community

RESOURCE 5.1

Dealing With the Anger of Parents

1. Have someone else present (teacher, administrator, etc.)

2. Offer them a seat in a private setting; get off your feet

3. Wait and listen

4. Do not become defensive; watch tone of voice

5. Speak softly, slowly, remain calm, and be aware of your posture

6. Show genuine interest in the student and express this

7. Do not fear anger, but understand its origins

8. Try to determine the cause of the anger

9. Sometimes suggest a later meeting time

10. Use phrases that are placating

11. Not all parents are going to leave feeling good

12. Acknowledge their anger and convey concern

13. Avoid using angry responses, sarcasm, or negative nonverbal clues

14. Seek assistance or support from principal or counselor

Placating Responses

- "I feel uncomfortable discussing this now. Could we set up a time we could meet that would be . . ."
- "I can appreciate how frustrating . . ."
- "We are here to help your child and have only his (her) best interest at heart."
- "Let me see if I understand what you are concerned about."
- "What do you want me to do? How do you want me to accomplish this?" Follow with "What can we do together?"

Source: Morehead, 2001.

RESOURCE 5.2

Parent Tips for Conference Preparation

Before the Conference:

1. Make arrangements for your other children, if necessary. The conference is for you and your child's teacher; small children can be distracting and take time away from the discussion.

2. Jot down any questions you may have for the teacher, such as
   - Is my child working to the best of his (her) ability?
   - How is he (or she) progressing in reading, math, handwriting, and other subjects?
   - Does he (or she) get along well with teachers and children?
   - Does he (or she) follow classroom rules?
   - What are his (or her) attitudes in class?
   - How do you handle (specific behavior)?
   - What do the tests say about his (or her) ability?

3. Talk to your child about the conference. Ask if he or she wants you to ask any questions or voice any concerns.

4. Collect any records or information that may help the teacher. Try to anticipate questions and prepare answers.

At the Conference:

1. Please be on time and stay only for your scheduled time. You may schedule another conference if you do not cover all the necessary information in the allotted time.

2. Discuss only the child at issue. Try not to stray off the subject. Do not bring up your other children's problems.

3. Ask any questions about your child's education. Advocate for your child. Know your child's rights.

4. Volunteer information that may help the teacher plan programming for your child.

5. Feel free to take notes to review later.

After the Conference:

Feel free to contact your child's teacher for further clarification.

Source: Shea & Bauer, 1991, p. 146.

RESOURCE 5.3

Web Sites for the School Community

Alcohol and Substance Abuse

Al-Anon/Al-Ateen
http://www. al-anon-alateen.org

Safe and Drug-Free Schools
    Program
U.S. Department of Education
http://www.ed.gov/about/offices/
list/osdfs/index.html

Substance Abuse and Mental
Health Services Administration
http://www.samhsa.gov/

The Web of Addictions
http://www.well.com/user/woa/

Career Resources

AES Education Planning Center
http://www.aessuccess.org/
getting/ index.shtml

America's Career Infonet
http://www.acinet.org/acinet/

Career Experience
http://www. careerexperience
.com/

Career Key
http://www. careerkey.org/
cgi-bin/ck.pl? action=choices

Career Magazine
http://www. careermag.com/

Career Pathways—American
Student Achievement Institute
http://asai.indstate.edu/guiding
allkids/careerpathways.htm

Career Planning Resource Center
http://www.learning4liferesources
.com

Careerbuilder
http://www.careerbuilder.com/

Hot Jobs for the 21st Century
http://stats.bls.gov/emp/emptab3
.htm

Mapping Your Future
http://www.mapping-your-
future.org/

Monster Board
http://www.monster.com/

National Career Development
Association
http://ncda.org

Occupational Outlook Handbook
http://www.bls.gov/oco

O*NET, Occupational Information Network
http://www. doleta.gov/programs/onet/

The Real Game
http://www.realgame.com

The *Wall Street Journal* Executive Career Site
http://www. careerjournal.com/

What Color Is Your Parachute?
http://www.jobhuntersbible.com/

WorkTree.com Job Search Center
http://www.careerresource.com/

College Resources

American College Testing
http://www.act.org/

Business, Trade, and Technical Schools
http://www.rwm.org/rwm

College Board
http://www.collegeboard.org/

College Net
http://www.collegenet.com/

Historically Black Colleges and Universities Network
http://www.hbcunetwork.com

Kaplan Test Prep and Admissions
http://www.kaptest.com/

Mapping Your Future
http://www.mapping-your-future.org/planning

My College Guide
http://www.mycollegeguide.org/index.phtml

Petersons College Information
http://www.petersons.com/

Financial Aid Resources

AESmentor
http://www.aessuccess.org/getting/index.shtml

College Is Possible Campaign
http://www.collegeispossible.org/

College Opportunities On-Line (COOL)
http://www.nces.ed.gov/ipeds/cool/

FastWeb
http://www.fastweb.com/

FinAid! Guide to Financial Aid
http://www.finaid.org/

Financial Aid Need Estimator
http://www.act.org/fane/index.html

Free Application for Federal Student Aid
http://fafsa.ed.gov/

PHEAA Creating Access to Education
http://pheaa.org/

The Smart Student Guide to Financial Aid
http://www.finaid.org/

Mental Health Resources

Center for Mental Health Services
Knowledge Exchange Network
http://www.mentalhealth.org

Child Abuse Prevention Network
http://child-abuse.com/

Diagnosis, Research, and
Pharmaceutical Information
http://www.mentalhealth.com

Emotional and Behavior Problems
http://www.air-dc.org/cecp/

Facts for Families
http://www.aacap.org/info_
families/index.htm

Mental Health Matters
http://www.mental-health-
matters.com/

Reporting Child Abuse
http://www.kidsafe-caps.org/
report.html

Stress Management
http://www.stress.org

Suicide Prevention Action Network
http://www.spanusa.org/

The Federation of Families for
Children's Mental Health
http://www.ffcmh.org

Youth Suicide Prevention
http://www.spyc.sanpedro.com/
suicide.htm

Research Resources

Ask ERIC
http://www.eric.ed.gov

Federal No Child Left Behind
Act of 2001
http://www.ed.gov/nclb/
landing.jhtml#

The National Center for School
Counseling Outcome Research
http://www.umass.edu/school
counseling/

Violence Prevention

Blueprints for Violence Prevention
http://www.colorado.edu/cspv/
blueprints/index.html

Bullying: Facts For Schools and
Parents
http://www.naspcenter.org/
factsheets/bullying_fs.html

Coping With School Violence
http://search.familyeducation.com

Division of Violence Prevention
http://www.cdc.gov/ncipc/dvp/
dvp.htm

Early Warning, Timely Response:
A Guide to Safe Schools
http://www.athealth.com/Consu
mer/issues/early_warning.html

National Youth Gang Center
http://www.iir.com/nygc

School Safety and Legal Rights of
Students
http://www.ericdigests.org/
1998-2/safety.htm

Strategies to Reduce School
Violence
http://www.ericdigests.org/
1998-1/overview.htm

Web Sites for Parents

Early Childhood and Parenting Collaborative
http://ecap.crc.uiuc.edu/info/

Family Education
http://www.familyeducation.com/home/

Middle Web
http://www.middleweb.com

National Association of Partners in Education
http://www.napehq.org

Parents Count: Resources for Parents of
Middle School Students
http://www.parentscount.net/guidance/
detail.cfm?articleID=59

Parent Resource Center: At Risk Youth
Programs Help for Parents With Troubled Teen
http://www.parenthelpcenter.org/

Family and Parenting Resource
Center
http://www.learning4lifere
sour.com/parenting_1.html

Federal Resources for
Educational Excellence
http://www.ed.gov/free/

National Association for Gifted
Children
http://www.nagc.org

National Coalition for Parent
Involvement in Education
http://www.ncpie.org

Parents Know
http://www.parentsknow.com

Web Sites for Students

American Student Achievement
Institute 4-Year High School
Course Plans
http://asai.indstate.edu/guiding
allkids/4yrhscourseplan.htm

eSylvan Online Tutoring
http://www.esylvan.com/

Learning to Learn
http://www.ldrc.ca/projects/
projects.php?id=26#op

Resource Links for Middle
School Students
http://www.nc4h.org/greenlight/
kidlinks/links-ms.html

The Council for Exceptional Children
http://www.cec.sped.org/home.htm

Yellow Ribbon Suicide Prevention
Program
http://www.yellowribbon.org/

Hauppauge Middle School
http://www.hauppauge.k12.ny.us/
new%20web/web2/Middle%20
School/curriculumhs.htm

Learning Styles
http://www.learning4liferesources
.com/learning_style_1.html

Online Spanish Tutorial
Sponsored by:
http://www.LearnPlus.com/

Teen Learning Network
http://www.childadvocate.net

The English Tutor Online Tutoring
for High School Students
http://www.theenglishtutor.com/

FORM 5.1

Conducting a Successful Parent Conference

Pre-Conference Tasks

_____ Prior written notification of meeting given to the parents and other conference participants (at least seven working days in advance).

_____ Notification of meeting should include the following:

a. Date, time, and exact location of the conference

b. Purpose of conference

c. List of persons attending the conference and their respective positions (include parent's and student's name in the notification)

d. Request for confirmation of attendance from all invitees

e. Name, telephone number, and/or e-mail address of the person responsible for conducting the conference

_____ Select and reserve conference location. This location needs to be in a neutral area that is comfortable and free from interruptions, such as the school's main conference room.

_____ Formulate a meeting agenda and distribute to parents and all school personnel invited to the conference before the designated meeting date.

_____ Send parents a conference preparation handout (Resource 5.2).

_____ Telephone parents two days prior to conference as a friendly reminder.

_____ Remind school personnel two days prior to conference.

_____ Ensure the following school personnel have been invited to the conference:

a. **Progress Report Conference:** Parents, teachers, school counselor, and additional school personnel as requested or required.

b. **Problem-Solving Conference:** Parents, teachers, school administrator, school counselor, and additional school personnel as requested or required.

c. **IEP Conference:** Parents, at least one regular education teacher of inclusive students, special education teacher, school or special education administrator, related service providers, transition service providers, and the student (if appropriate).

FORM 5.1

Conducting a Successful Parent Conference (Continued)

Conference Tasks

_____ The school official in charge of the conference is responsible for:

a. Introductions of conference attendees

b. Providing a *Parent Rights* booklet to the parents before proceeding with an IEP Conference or Meeting.

c. Stating the purpose of the conference.

d. Designating someone to take minutes of the conference (Form 5.2).

e. Closing the conference by summarizing all information that was reviewed and discussed during the conference.

_____ All information discussed and strategies and plans developed during the conference should be written on a minutes page and signed by all attendees.

_____ Parents should be given a copy of the conference minutes.

Post-Conference Tasks

_____ Send parents a follow-up letter that includes the following:

a. Thank parents for attending the meeting.

b. Send any documents requested by the parents.

c. Advise parents of the best school hours and days to reach the conference contact person if they have further questions.

d. Conclude the letter with a positive comment.

FORM 5.2

Conference Minutes

Date: _____

Student Name: _____   Grade: _____

Conference Purpose:

_____**Academic Progress of Student:**
(Reading, Writing, English, Math, Science, Social Studies, other)
     a. Performance on tests
     b. Performance on quizzes
     c. Completion of homework
     d. Completion of projects

_____**Discipline Issues**
     a. Student self-control
     b. Student affect: enthusiasm, leadership, followership, responsibility, reactions
       to rewards and contingencies
     c. Social conventions: manners, courtesy, respect for others and their property

_____**Other:** _____

Proposed Strategies:

_____

_____

_____

Conference Summary:

_____

_____

_____

Conference Participants:

_____   _____   _____

_____   _____   _____

Best Practice 6

Design a Personal Plan for Professional Development

Best Practice 6: Design a Personal Plan for Professional Development

Professional development is essential in order for school counselors to keep pace with the advancements in the profession, to maintain professional competence, and to learn about current trends in the field of education. According to ASCA (2003), "professional and personal growth are ongoing throughout the counselor's career" (p. 125). Stephen Covey's "Habit 7: Sharpen the Saw" accurately depicts the need for school counselors to devise a personalized long-term professional development program. Covey (1992) states, "If you don't improve and renew yourself constantly, you'll fall into entropy, closed systems and styles. At one end of the continuum is entropy (everything breaks down), and at the other end is continuous improvement, innovation, and refinement" (p. 47). The school counseling profession has not been left untouched by the No Child Left Behind federal initiative, and school counselors have been thrust into the accountability arena. Counselors must arm themselves with the knowledge and skills necessary to prove how students are different as a result of their programs. In addition, the school counseling program should be an integral part of a school's instructional program and academic mission; therefore, school counselors have a responsibility to keep abreast of new instructional techniques, strategies, and programs that impact student learning and achievement. In this chapter, we provide information and resources to help the school counselor prepare a professional development plan. We suggest strategies and provide resources for developing appropriate plans for continued growth in the profession. At the end of the chapter is a reference list of professional associations, journals, books, and Web sites that will assist the school counselor to stay current in the profession.

School counselors should join at least one professional organization. Often these organizations publish informative magazines or newsletters, conduct annual state or national conferences, and provide members with liability insurance. School counselors should also attend at least one major conference a year. Professional conferences for educators typically follow a format that includes at least one general session with a keynote speaker, a variety of small-group sessions on specific topics, and numerous how-to workshops that engage participants in interactive learning activities. It's helpful to review all conference information in advance and plan a daily agenda that will maximize the conference experience. Conference brochures can often be obtained in advance by visiting the sponsoring organization's Web site. Conferences can be viewed as one-stop resource centers that provide numerous opportunities to exchange ideas, materials, and resources with other practicing counselors and possibly obtain staff development or continuing education credit. Staff development credit can be used for recertification in some states. Form 6.1 is a conference planning guide that can be used to ensure that the school counselor maximizes his or her opportunities and time at any conference.

The following forms are found in this section:

Form 6.1 Conference Planning Guide

School counselors should read professional journals and books that pertain to the school counseling profession or to education. These resources are available to faculty and staff members in the media centers of most schools. However, if your school's media center is lacking in a particular area, check with the media specialist to see if additional resources can be ordered. Finally, school counselors should enroll in advanced college courses or local staff development classes offered through the school system. College courses are usually more expensive; however, these courses can be applied toward an additional degree or area of certification. Typically, staff development classes are offered at low or no cost to school employees, are scheduled after school hours or during the summer, and give credit toward recertification.

We recommend that the school counselor begin developing a professional development plan prior to the beginning of each new school year (see Form 6.2). The plan should include short- and long-range professional goals, a timeline for goal completion, and the school counselor's particular areas of interest. In addition, the plan should include any staff development or training the school counselor needs to effectively perform his or her current job or contribute to a school's program initiatives. A completed professional development plan can help the school counselor to perform a self-assessment at the end of each school year, and it provides a record of professional pursuits and activities over a period of time. The plan should be placed in the school counselor's portfolio at the end of each school year (see Form 6.3).

The following forms are found in this section:

Form 6.2 Professional Development Plan

Form 6.3 A Professional Portfolio for School Counselors

Professional development is a continuous process and an individual responsibility. In a time when teachers across the country are being held under a high-powered microscope, school counselors are finding their programs and services are being scrutinized for productivity and effectiveness in the same manner. Counselors who constantly "sharpen the saw" will find themselves to be on the cutting edge of the profession and in a constant state of professional and personal growth.

The following forms are found in this section:

Resource 6.1: The Secondary School Counselor's Guide to Professional Organizations

Resource 6.2: The Secondary School Counselor's Guide to Professional Periodicals

Resource 6.3: The Secondary School Counselor's Guide to Professional Books

Resource 6.4: Web Sites for School Counselors

RESOURCE 6.1

The Secondary School Counselor's Guide to Professional Organizations

American Association of School Personnel Administrators (AASPA)
http://www.aaspa.org/search.html

American Counseling Association
http://www.counseling.org/

American School Counselor Association
http://www.schoolcounselor.org/

American Vocational Association
http://www.avaonline.olrg/index.html

Association for Assessment in Counseling
http://www.aac.ncat.edu./

Association for Career & Technical Education (ACTE)
http://www.acteonline.org/

Association for Counselor Education and Supervision
http://www.acesonline.net/home.html

Association for Multicultural Counseling and Development
http://www.nu.edu/multicultural/amcd.html

Council for Accreditation of Counseling and Related Educational Programs
http://www.counseling.org/cacrep

Drug Abuse Resistance Education
http://www.dare-america.com/

Institution of Career Guidance
http://www.icg-uk.org/

National Board for Certified Counselors
http://www.nbcc.org

National Career Development Association
http://www.ncda.org/

National Educational Association
http://www.nea.org

National Foundation for the Improvement of Education
http://www.nfie.org

National Mental Health Association
http://www.nmha.org/

National Middle School Association
http://www.nmsa.org/

National Peer Helper Association
http://www.peerhelping.org/

The Association for Addiction Professionals-NAADAC
http://www.naadac.org/

The Character Education Institute
http://www.cup.edu/education/charactered/

RESOURCE 6.2

The Secondary School Counselor's Guide to Professional Periodicals

Adolescence
Libra Publishers, Inc.
3089C Clairemont Dr.,
Suite 383
San Diego, CA 92117
Telephone: (619) 571-1414
Publishing schedule: quarterly
Cost: $75.00

American Journal of Art Therapy
Frances F. Kaplan, Editor
American Art Therapy Association, Inc.
1202 Allanson Rd.
Mundelein, IL 60060-3808
Telephone: (847) 949-6064
Toll-free: (888) 290-0878
Fax: (847) 566-4580
E-mail: info@arttherapy.org
Publishing schedule: quarterly
Cost: $30.00

American Journal of Education
William Lowe Boyd, Editor
200 Rackley Building
Penn State University
University Park, PA 16802
E-mail: ajed@psu.edu
Publishing schedule: quarterly
Cost: $36.00

American Secondary Education
James A. Rycik, Editor
Ashland University Weltmer Center
401 College Avenue
Ashland, OH 44805-3702
Telephone: (419) 289-5273
Fax: (419) 289-5333
E-mail: gvanderz@ashland.edu
Publishing schedule: three times a year
Cost: $30.00

The Attention Deficit Hyperactivity
Disorders Report
Russell A. Barkley, Editor
Guilford Publications, Inc.
72 Spring Street
New York, NY 10012
Telephone: (212) 431-9800
Toll-free: (800) 365-7006
Fax: (212) 966-6708
E-mail: info@guilford.com
Publishing schedule: six times a year
Cost: $79.00

Campus Opportunities for Students With
Learning Differences
Octameron Associates
P.O. Box 2748
Alexandria, VA 22301
Telephone: (703) 836-5480
Fax: (703) 836-5650
E-mail: info@octameron.com
Cost: $5.00

Career Development for Exceptional
Individuals
Council for Exceptional Children
1110 North Glebe Road
Arlington, VA 22201-5704
Telephone: (703) 620-3660
Toll-free: (888) CEC-SPED
Fax: (703) 264-9494
E-mail: service@cec.sped.org
Publishing Schedule: twice a year
Cost: $15.00

Career Development Quarterly
Mark Pope, Editor
Division of Counseling and Family
Therapy
College of Education
University of Missouri
415 Marillae Hall
One University Boulevard
St. Louis, MO 63121-4499
Telephone: (314) 516-7121
Fax: (314) 516-5784
E-mail: pope@umsl.edu
Publishing schedule: quarterly
Cost: $55.00

Counseling and Values
Dennis W. Engels, Editor
Stovall Hall 155
Box 311337
University of North Texas
Denton, TX 76203-1337
Telephone: (940) 565-2918
Fax: (940) 565-2905
E-mail: engels@coefs.coe.unt.edu
Publishing schedule: three
times a year
Cost: $41.00

Counselor Education and Supervision
Marlowe H. Smaby, Editor
University of Nevada
Department of Counseling and
Educational Psychology
Mail Stop 281
Reno, NV 89557-0213
Telephone (775) 784-1772
Fax: (775) 784-1990
E-mail: smaby@unr.edu
Publishing schedule: quarterly
Cost: $70.00

Educating At-Risk Youth
Janet Simon, Editor
National Professional Resources
P.O. Box 1479
Port Chester, NY 10573
Telephone: (914) 937-8879
Publishing schedule: ten times a year
Cost: $68.00

Education and Treatment of Children
Bernard Fabry, Editor
The Roscoe Ledger
P.O. Box 536
Chester and Latta Streets
Roscoe, PA 15477
Telephone: (724) 938-9495
Fax: (724) 938-9111
E-mail: bdfabry@aol.com
Publishing schedule: quarterly
Cost: $45.00

Educational Leadership
Margaret M. Scherer, Editor
ASCD
1703 North Beauregard Street
Alexandria, VA 22311-1714
Telephone: (703) 578-9600
Toll-free: (800) 933-2723
Fax: (703) 575-5400
E-mail: el@ascd.org
Publishing schedule: eight times a year
Cost: $36.00

High School Journal
Howard N. Machtinger, Editor
University of North Carolina Press
116 South Boundary Street
Chapel Hill, NC 27514-3808
Telephone: (919) 966-3561, ext. 256
Toll-free: (800) 848-6224
Fax: (800) 272-6817, ext. 256
E-mail: uncpress_journals@unc.edu
Publishing schedule: quarterly
Cost: $30.00

Journal for Vocational Special Needs
Education
John Gugerty, Editor
Center for Education and Work
University of Wisconsin
1025 W. Johnson Street
Madison, WI 53706-1796
Telephone: (608) 263-2724
Fax: (608) 262-3050
E-mail: jgugerty@education.wisc.edu
Publishing schedule: three times a year
Cost: $48.00

Journal of Adolescent and Adult Literacy
F. Todd Goodson, Editor
International Reading Association
800 Barksdale Road
Newark, DE 19714-8139
Telephone: (302) 731-1600
Fax: (302) 731-1057
E-mail: tgoodson@ksu.edu
Publishing schedule: eight times a year
Cost: $61.00

Journal of Alcohol and Drug Education
Manoj Sharma, Editor
School of HPER
University of Nebraska at Omaha
Omaha, NE 68182-0216
Telephone: (402) 554-2670
Fax: (402) 554-3693
E-mail: msharma@mail.unomaha.edu
Publishing schedule: three times a year
Cost: $45.00

Journal of Applied School Psychology
Charles A. Maher, Editor
Rutgers University
152 Frelinghuysen Road, Suite A305
Piscataway, NJ 08854
Telephone: (732) 445-2000
E-mail: camaher@rci.rutgers.edu
Publishing schedule: twice a year
Cost: $60.00

Journal of Career Development
Norman C. Gysbers, Editor
Kluwer Academic Publishers
101 Philip Drive
Assinippi Park
Nowell, MA 02061
Telephone: (781) 871-6600
Fax: (781) 871-6528
E-mail: Kluwer@wkap.com
Publishing schedule: quarterly
Cost: $58.00

Journal of Career Planning and
Employment
National Association of Colleges and
Employers
62 Highland Avenue
Bethlehem, PA 18017-9805
Fax: (610) 868-0208
Internet: www.naceweb.org
Publishing schedule: quarterly
Cost: $72.00

Journal of Counseling and Development
A. Scott McGowan, Editor
Department of Counseling and
Development
Long Island University
C.W. Post Campus
720 Northern Boulevard
Brookville, NY 11548-1300
Telephone: (516) 299-2815
Fax: (516) 299-3312
E-mail: amcgowan@liu.edu
Publishing schedule: quarterly
Cost: $152.00

Journal of Drug Education
James Robinson, Editor
Baywood Publishing Company, Inc.
26 Austin Ave.
Box 337
Amityville, NY 11701
Telephone: (631) 691-1270
Toll-free: (800) 638-7819
Fax: (631) 691-1770
E-mail: info@baywood.com
Publishing schedule: quarterly
Cost: $67.00

Journal of Multicultural Counseling and
Development
    Gargi Roysircar-Sodowsky, Editor
    Department of Clinical Psychology
    Antioch New England Graduate School
    40 Avon Street
    Keene, NH 03431-3516
    Telephone: (603) 357-3122
    Fax: (603) 357-0718
    E-mail: g_roysircar_sodowsky@
    antiochne.edu
    Publishing schedule: quarterly
    Cost: $69.00

Journal of Research in Childhood
Education
    Kathleen Glascott Burriss, Editor
    Department of Elementary and Special
    Education
    Box 69
    Middle Tennessee State University
    Murgreesboro, TN 37132
    Publishing schedule: twice a year
    Cost: $79.00

Journal of Vocational Education Research
    James R. Stone, Editor
    University of Minnesota
    1954 Buford Hall
    St. Paul, MN 55108
    Telephone: (]612) 624-1795
    Fax: (612) 624-4720
    E-mail: stone003@tc.umn.edu
    Publishing schedule: quarterly
    Cost: $57.00

Measurement and Evaluation in
Counseling and Development
    Patricia B. Elmore, Editor
    College of Education and Human
    Services
    Dean's Office—Mailcode 4624
    Southern Illinois University
    Carbondale, IL 62901-4624
    Telephone: (618) 453-2415
    Fax: (618) 453-1646
    E-mail: pbelmore@siu.edu
    Publishing schedule: quarterly
    Cost: $63.00

NACADA Journal
    Gary M. Padak and Terry L. Kuhn,
    Co-Editors
    Kansas State University
    2323 Anderson Avenue, Suite 225
    Manhattan, KS 66502-2912
    Telephone: (785) 532-5717
    Fax: (785) 532-7732
    E-mail: nacada@ksu.edu
    Publishing schedule: twice a year
    Cost: $50.00

National Forum of Teacher Education
Journal (NFTE Journal)
    William Kritsonis, Editor
    National Forum Journals
    P.O. Box 7400
    Lake Charles, LA 70605-7400
    Telephone: (337) 477-0008
    Fax: (337) 480-3663
    E-mail: WAkritsonis@aol.com
    Publishing schedule: twice a year
    Cost: $44.00

Phi Delta Kappan
    Bruce M. Smith, Editor
    408 North Union, Box 789
    Bloomington, IN 47402-0789
    Telephone: (812) 339-1156
    E-mail: kappan@pdkintl.org
    Publishing schedule: ten times a year
    Cost: $39.00

Preventing School Failure
    Heldref Publications
    1319 Eighteenth Street Northwest
    Washington, DC 20036-1802
    Telephone: (202) 296-6267
    Fax: (202) 296-5149
    E-mail: psf@heldref.org
    Publishing schedule: quarterly
    Cost: $45.00

Professional School Counseling
American School Counselor
Association Subscription Office
P.O. Box 830409
Birmingham, AL 35283
Telephone: (800) 633-4931
Fax: (205) 995-1588
E-mail: asca@ebsco.com
Publishing schedule: five times a year
Cost: $90.00

Psychology in the Schools
LeAdelle Phelps, Editor
Department of Counseling, School,
and Educational Psychology
State University of New York, Buffalo
409 Baldy Hall
Buffalo, NY 14260-1000
Telephone: (716) 645-2484, ext. 1055
Fax: (716) 645-6616
E-mail: phelps@buffalo.edu
Publishing schedule: eight times a year
Cost: $95.00

Reading Improvement
Phil Feldman, Editor
Project Innovation, Inc.
P.O. Box 8508 Spring Hill Station
Mobile, AL 36689-0826
Telephone: (251) 633-7802
Fax: (251) 639-7360
E-mail: pfeldman@gulftel.com
Publishing schedule: quarterly
Cost: $34.00

Rehabilitation Counseling Bulletin
Douglas C. Strohmer, Editor
LSU Health Sciences Center
School of Allied Health Professions
Department of Rehabilitation
Counseling
1900 Gravier Street, Room 8C1,
Box G6-2
New Orleans, LA 70112-2262
Telephone: (504) 568-4315
Fax: (504) 568-4324
E-mail: sdstroh@communique.net
Publishing schedule: quarterly
Cost: $44.00

Techniques: Connecting Education and
Careers
Association for Career and Technical
Education
1410 King Street
Alexandria, VA 22314
Telephone: (703) 683-3111
Fax: (703) 683-7424
E-mail: techniques@acteonline.org
Publishing schedule: eight times
a year
Cost: $48.00

RESOURCE 6.3

The Secondary School Counselor's
Guide to Professional Books

Title: *A Survival Guide for the Elementary/Middle School Counselor (2nd ed.)*
Author: John J. Schmidt
Publisher: John Wiley & Sons
Date: February 2004

Title: *Memoirs of a Middle School Counselor*
Author: D. Jean Lang
Publisher: Trafford Publishing
Date: July 2003

Title: *Counseling Today's Secondary Students: Practical Strategies,*
Techniques and Materials for the School Counselor
Author: Kenneth Hitchner
Publisher: John Wiley & Sons
Date: October 2002

Title: *The School Counselor's Book of Lists*
Author: Dorothy J. Blum
Publisher: John Wiley & Sons
Date: September 2002

Title: *School Counselor*
Author: Kenneth Hitchner
Publisher: John Wiley & Sons
Date: May 2002

Title: *School Counselor's Letter Book*
Author: Kenneth Hitchner
Publisher: John Wiley & Sons
Date: May 2002

Title: *School Counselor's Scrapbook: A Collection of Bulletin Boards, Small*
Group Activities, Arts, Crafts and Creative Props
Author: Janet M. Bender
Publisher: Younglight
Date: January 2002

Title: *Transition Planning for Secondary Students With Disabilities*
Author: Robert W. Flexer, Thomas J. Simmons, Pamela Luft, Robert Baer
Publisher: Prentice Hall PTR
Date: September 2000

Title: *Caring for Kids in Communities: Using Mentorship, Peer Support, and Student Leadership Programs in Schools*
Author: Julia Ellis
Publisher: Peter Lang
Date: July 2001

Title: *Buddies: Reading, Writing and Math Lessons*
Author: Pia Hansen Powell
Publisher: Eye on Education
Date: January 2001

Title: *Tutoring Programs for Struggling Readers: The America Reads Challenge*
Author: Lesley Mandel Morrow
Publisher: Guilford Publications
Date: November 2000

Title: *Adolescent Lives in Transition: How Social Class Influences the Adjustment to Middle School*
Author: Donna Maria San Antonio
Publisher: State University of New York Press
Date: February 2004

Title: *Cultivating Kindness in School: Activities That Promote Integrity, Respect and Compassion in Elementary and Middle School Students*
Author: Ric Stuecker
Publisher: Research Press
Date: 2003

Title: *Student Transitions from Middle to High School: Improving Achievement and Creating a Safer Environment*
Author: J. Allen Queen
Publisher: Eye on Education
Date: February 2002

Title: *In Our Own Words: Students' Perspectives on School*
Author: Jeffrey J. Shultz
Publisher: Rowman & Littlefield
Date: October 2001

Title: *Middle School: The Real Deal: From Cafeteria to Combination Locks*
Author: Juliana Farrell
Publisher: Morrow/Avon
Date: April 2001

Title: *Banishing Anonymity: Middle and High School Advisement Programs*
Authors: John M. Jenkins and Bonnie S. Daniel
Publisher: Eye on Education
Date: January 2000

Title: *Transforming Learning for the Workplace of the New Millennium*
Author: Eleni Roulis
Publisher: Scarecrow Press
Date: January 2004

Title: *School Counseling: Foundations and Contemporary Issues*
Author: Daniel T. Sciarra
Publisher: Wadsworth
Date: October 2003

Title: *School-Based Interventions: The Tools You Need to Succeed*
Authors: Kathleen L. Lane et al.
Publisher: Allyn & Bacon
Date: September 2003

Title: *School Counseling for the Twenty-First Century*
Authors: Stanley B. Baker et al.
Publisher: Prentice Hall PTR
Date: August 2003

Title: *Standards-Based Counseling in the Middle School*
Author: Mary Ellen Davis
Publisher: 1st Books Library
Date: November 2002

Title: *From Advisory to Advocacy: Meeting Every Student's Needs*
Authors: Michael James et al.
Publisher: National Middle School Association
Date: March 2002

Title: *Dropping Out or Hanging In: What You Should Know Before Dropping Out of School*
Author: Duane Brown
Publisher: McGraw-Hill Trade
Date: 2003

Title: *School Counseling in the Secondary School: A Comprehensive Process and Program*
Authors: Colette T. Dollarhide et al.
Publisher: Allyn & Bacon
Date: October 2002

Title: *A Practical Guide to Working With Parents*
Authors: Christine Hobart et al.
Publisher: Nelson Thornes
Date: September 2003

Title: *Counseling Toward Solutions: A Practical Solution-Focused Program for Working With Students, Teachers, and Parents*
Author: Linda Metcalf
Publisher: John Wiley & Sons
Date: September 2002

Title: *Places for Struggling Teens 2002/2003*
Author: Lon Woodbury
Publisher: Woodbury Reports
Date: 2002

RESOURCE 6.4

Web Sites for School Counselors

Professional Resources

ACA Ethical Guidelines
http://www.counseling.org/

All Kids Grieve
http://allkidsgrieve.org/

Army Deployment Handbook: Resource for Helping Students With
War Anxieties
http://www.wood.army.mil/mwr/deploymenthndbook.htm

Association for Assessment in Counseling and Education
http://aac.ncat.edu/

Association for Counselor Education and Supervision
http://www.acesonline.net

The Counselor Education Department at California University of
Pennsylvania: Links
http://www.cup.edu/graduate/counsed/LINKS.HTM

DSM-IV
http://www.dr-bob.org/tips/dsm4a.html

Education Trust Transforming School Counseling
http://www2.edtrust.org/EdTrust/Transforming%2BSchool%2
Bcounseling

The Guidance Channel
http://www.guidancechannel.com/default.asp

Journal of Technology in Counseling
http://jtc.colstate.edu/

Middle School Students and School Life
http://www.middleweb.com/ContntsStudn.html

National Education Association Crisis Communications and Toolkit
http://www.nea.org/crisis/

National Educational Service
http://www.nesonline.com

Peer Resources
http://www.peer.ca/peer.html

Professional Resources for School Counselors
http://www.school-counselors.com

Quick Training Aid: School-Based Crisis Intervention
http://smhp.psych.ucla.edu/qf/crisis_qt/

Safeguarding Your Children at School: Helping Children Deal With a
School Bully
http://www.pta.org/programs/sycsch.htm

U.S. Department of Education
http://www.ed.gov

Research Resources

Center for School Counseling Outcome Research
http://www.umass.edu/schoolcounseling/

Counseling Outfitters
http://www.counselingoutfitters.com

Education Resources Information Center (ERIC)
http://www.eric.ed.gov

Federal No Child Left Behind Act of 2001
http://www.ed.gov/nclb/landing.jhtml#

FORM 6.1

Conference Planning Guide

Conference Name: _____

Conference Dates: _____

Conference Location: _____

Sponsoring Organization: _____

Conference Cost: $_____

1. Registration Fee: $_____

2. Hotel Accommodations: $_____

3. Travel/Mileage: $_____

   TOTAL EXPENSE: $_____

   Conference Theme or Objectives:

1. _____

2. _____

3. _____

4. _____

5. _____

PERSONAL CONFERENCE SCHEDULE

DATE	TIME	SESSION TITLE	LOCATION

FORM 6.2

Professional Development Plan

School Year: _____

School Counselor: _____

Certification Number: _____   Expiration Date: _____

Licensure Number: _____   Expiration Date: _____

Certification Area/Grade Level: _____

Short-Range Professional Goals (Completion Within One Year):

Professional Goals	Completion Date
1.	
2.	
3.	
4.	
5.	

Long-Range Professional Goals (Completion Within Five Years):

Professional Goals	Completion Date
1.	
2.	
3.	
4.	
5.	

FORM 6.3

A Professional Portfolio for School Counselors

A professional portfolio is essential for all school counselors who are seeking employment or documenting personal growth in the field. The portfolio is a tool for showcasing personal attributes, skills, and activities; it highlights one's accomplishments as a school counselor and professional educator. Electronic portfolios are becoming more popular due to the convenience of the Internet and the ease with which Web page portfolios can be modified and updated. We recommend that the reader update and review the portfolio regularly and reflect on the artifacts collected throughout his or her journey.

Portfolio Contents

1. Cover Page	7. Descriptions of Special Projects or Programs
2. Table of Contents	8. Technology Applications and Skills
3. Personal Résumé	9. Professional Development Activities
4. Philosophy of Counseling and Education	10. Copy of Awards or Certificates
5. Graduate Coursework	11. Copy of Certification and/or Licensures
6. Internship and Practicum Experiences	12. Copy of Letters of Recommendation

Portfolio Tips

A school counselor's professional portfolio should:

1. be placed in a three-ring notebook with dividers or tabs.

2. be neat, clean, well-organized, and have a consistent appearance.

3. contain only copies of important documents, in case an interviewer wants to keep it.

4. contain current information, just like a résumé.

Appendix A

Stress Management for Secondary School Counselors

To live and work in today's society is to have stress. Seaward defined stress "as the inability to cope with a perceived or real (or imaginary) threat to one's mental, physical, emotional, and spiritual well-being [sic] which results in a series of physiological responses" (Massey, 1998, p. 1). The simple definition of stress is the body's reaction to the demands placed upon it. A certain amount of stress is helpful to keep individuals focused on the job or problem; however, too much pressure may cause personal distress and loss of job efficiency. The key issue seems to be how the individual perceives and responds to the stress rather than the amount of personal pressure.

What are the sources of occupational stress for school counselors? In a review of empirical studies related to counselor stress, Morrissette (2000) discovered the following:

- Three Areas of Stress
  1. Quantitative Overload (little time to see students, huge caseloads)
  2. Role Conflict (too many clerical duties, too much paperwork)
  3. Role Ambiguity (lack of clarity concerning the counselor's role)

- Six Major Factors Comprising Stress
  1. Lack of Decision-Making Authority
  2. Financial Stress
  3. Responsible for Extraneous Duties

    4. Professional Job Overload

    5. Relationships With Teachers

    6. Relationships With Principals

- Three Areas of Stressful Events

    1. Harm or Loss

    2. Anticipatory Threat

    3. Challenge (p. 4)

School counselors can readily identify specific stressors under each of the general areas that Morrissette mentioned. Another area of potential stress for the school counselor is the anticipation of emotional distress engendered by becoming absorbed in the emotional hurt of their counselees. Other specific stressors for school counselors include the following:

1. Lack of materials, resources, and equipment

2. Lack of leadership and support

3. Excessive pressure from parents and community

4. Isolated counselor—no network of counselors available for support

5. No balance between school and personal life

How do school counselors manage occupational stress? Morrissette (2000) has suggested developing a plan of action that consists of three strategies: self-supervision, maintaining a support network, and mental health consultation (p. 8). In the self-supervision model, the school counselor identifies personal issues (e.g., fears, anxieties, and disappointments) that may impact job performance and the counselor-counselee relationship through scheduled times of reflection and deliberation. Another way of coping with work stress is to develop a network of colleagues, friends, and family with whom the professional can share experiences while maintaining confidentiality. The reward for expressing to this network of friends the challenges and risks involved in counseling is the important feedback and support that the school counselor receives. The third strategy is to seek mental health consultation; however, "counselors are often reluctant to discuss their emotional pain, fearing that others will equate their despair with incompetence, which will jeopardize their professional status" (p. 8). In combating personal and work-related stressors, the individual must examine the personal perceptions of the problem. Of course, this process involves reflection on the person's thoughts and beliefs in relation to the problem and the stressors.

- Schedule moments of reflection and stress management daily. Rise early and allow more time for personal reflection before work day begins.

- Recognize stressful situations quickly, analyze personal feelings, breathe deeply, and loosen muscles.
- When stress builds, use deep breathing techniques and progressive muscle relaxation exercises to reduce tension.
- Learn the strategies of conflict management.
- Develop and post a daily or weekly calendar of appointments to reduce interruptions or outside pressures of non-counseling duties.
- Learn and be willing to say "No."
- Ask for help.
- Focus on an immediate goal and work on it until it is completed.
- Try a new activity.
- Talk to significant other.
- Pay attention to health, diet, and sleep needs.
- Exercise daily.

Appendix B

Writing Effective Letters of Recommendation

The task of writing letters of recommendation for students is one that the secondary school counselor will encounter repeatedly throughout his or her career. The most common requests are from students nominated for school and community awards, applying to postsecondary institutions, competing for scholarships, and entering the workforce. An effective letter of recommendation, for most students, highlights academic performance, emphasizes positive character traits, conveys anecdotes that relate the counselor's personal interactions with the student, reveals how a student has overcome obstacles, and demonstrates the student's work ethic. Each letter should be unique and provide the reader with a true picture of the student. The counselor should schedule one or two interviews with students with whom they have had minimum interaction, in order to obtain the necessary information to write an effective recommendation. School counselors must remember that "a recommendation is an endorsement: 'Yes, this person would be an excellent candidate for your program'" (Maggio, 2001, p. 314). In addition, the reader must note that students have the legal right to see all letters written unless they waive that right.

We begin this section with a student recommendation worksheet that will assist the counselor to gather basic information about the student (Appendix D). Next, we have created a school profile worksheet that contains basic information about the student's school (Appendix E). Often postsecondary admissions officers and recruiters for collegiate athletic programs request a school profile to accompany all student information. Finally, the reader will find that the remainder of this section contains a list of tips for writing effective letters of recommendation (Appendix F); a word bank of adjectives (Appendix G); and five sample letters that can be customized to a student's particular situation, circumstance, or need (Appendix H).

Form B.1

STUDENT RECOMMENDATION WORKSHEET

Directions: Complete the Student Recommendation Worksheet using official student and school records.

Student Name: _____ Grade: _____

Program of Study (High School Students): _____

Grade Point Average: _____ Class Rank: _____

Attendance Record: _____

Discipline Record: _____

School Clubs/Organizations: _____

_____

_____

Community Clubs/Organizations: _____

_____

_____

Student Awards: _____

_____

Student Accomplishments: _____

_____

_____

Form B.2

SCHOOL PROFILE

Directions: The information needed to complete the school profile may be obtained from official school records or a current state report card.

School Name: _____

School Address: _____

_____

_____

Telephone Number: _____ Fax Number: _____

Web Address: _____

School Population: _____

School Classification for Athletic Competition: _____

School Grading Scale: _____

Programs of Study Offered: _____

_____

Special Academic Programs: _____

_____

Average SAT Score: _____ Average ACT Score: _____

Total Number of Graduates from Previous Year: _____

Total Number of Graduates Attending Postsecondary Institutions: _____

Unique School Characteristics: _____

_____

_____

Resource B.3

TIPS FOR WRITING
EFFECTIVE LETTERS OF RECOMMENDATION

TIP 1   The best recommendations present information in a passionate way. Be careful of becoming too subjective.

TIP 2   Make every student profile unique. Interview the student for information (inspiration) as necessary. Generic letters of any type are a waste of time. Even generic phrases should be avoided.

TIP 3   Keep your writing brief and to the point. There's no need to be flowery. A half page of clean and concise student analysis is excellent, and you don't need more than a full page.

TIP 4   Use present voice whenever possible, and keep the verbs active. Remember, the student typically has not yet graduated.

TIP 5   Avoid laundry lists of any type. Focus instead on one or two specific activities or anecdotes that illustrate some important aspect of the student's character.

TIP 6   Take the time to check for "red flags" in the student's record—anything that you would question if you were an admissions officer. Address those issues as necessary.

Source: Minnesota Higher Education Services Office, n.d.

Resource B.4

WORD BANK OF ADJECTIVES

admirable	effective	integrity	resourceful
approve	efficient	intelligent	respect
capable	endorse	invaluable	responsible
commendable	energetic	inventive	self-motivated
competent	ethical	loyal	sensible
congenial	excellent	meticulous	successful
conscientious	experienced	outstanding	suitable
considerate	first-rate	personable	tactful
cooperative	hardworking	praiseworthy	thoughtful
creative	honest	productive	trustworthy
dependable	imaginative	professional	valuable
diligent	indispensable	recommend	
discreet	ingenious	reliable	
dynamic	initiative	remarkable	

Source: Maggio, 2001, p. 318.

Resource B.5a

SAMPLE LETTERS

SAMPLE LETTER 1

December 12, 200X

Dear Dr. Davis:

It is a pleasure to recommend Robert Benson for admission to Mountain Laurel College. He is currently a senior in good standing at Jackson High School and demonstrates a high degree of motivation and enthusiasm in the classroom and extracurricular activities. I have served as his school counselor for the past four years.

Robert constantly challenges himself academically, as evidenced by his decision to complete the College Preparatory Program of Study with Distinction. He has a cumulative average of 90.132 and he is currently on track to be an honor graduate. This achievement is significant and indicative of his character and self-discipline. In addition, he communicates effectively with people from diverse backgrounds.

Robert is achievement motivated and goal oriented. His personal attributes of self-discipline, honesty, responsibility, and cooperative attitude will enable him to be successful in college and life.

Sincerely,

Charlene Weston

School Counselor

Jackson High School

Resource B.5b

SAMPLE LETTER 2

May 16, 200X

Dear Mr. Wells:

Amanda Springs has been enrolled in Pine Valley High School for two years and has earned only 2.5 credits. As her school counselor for two years, I am recommending her for the Job Corps. At age 17, she is uncomfortable in a ninth-grade homeroom, and struggles to earn credit necessary for graduation. She is motivated to pursue other options that would enrich her life and provide her with competencies necessary for independent living.

Amanda is a kind and gentle young lady searching for some direction in her life. She is quiet, but determined. In my opinion, Job Corps provides the best opportunity for her to acquire the skills and education needed for her to be self-sufficient. I believe that she would work diligently and prove to be successful if given the chance. She needs a fresh start in a new environment—something that Job Corps specializes in providing.

I hope that you will give serious consideration to accepting Amanda into your program. Please feel free to contact me if you need any further information.

Sincerely,

Ellen Newberry

School Counselor

Pine Valley High School

Resource B.5c

SAMPLE LETTER 3

May 3, 200X

Dear Mrs. Shoemaker:

It is a pleasure to recommend Charles T. Washington to you for an entry-level position in your company. He is a senior in good standing at Jefferson High School and will graduate with a Technical Career Diploma on May 18, 200X. In the four years that I have known him he has been elected treasurer of his class each year, demonstrating his honesty and trustworthiness.

Charles has worked diligently to complete his graduation requirements. Although he is weak in reading comprehension skills, he has a cumulative "B" average for the four years of high school. Charles has demonstrated positive character traits. For example, he attends school regularly, completing three years of perfect attendance, and completes his assignments on schedule. He also helps with the children's choir at the Mount Pleasant Baptist Church.

Charles has the skills and attitude to be successful in the workplace. He serves as an excellent role model for his peers, and I am glad to recommend him for a job.

Sincerely,

C. C. Birchfield

School Counselor

Jefferson High School

Resource B.5d

SAMPLE LETTER 4

April 16, 200X

Dear Mr. Hill:

It is a pleasure to recommend Susan Bridges, a senior of Martinez High School, for the Smith Funeral Home Scholarship. She is an outstanding young woman committed to graduating with honors. It has been my privilege to be her school counselor for four years.

Academically, Susan is completing the challenging College Preparatory with Distinction Plus program of study. She has a cumulative grade average of 90.687, allowing her to be an honor graduate. This achievement is significant when you consider that last year she missed being a junior honor student by one point; therefore, she worked diligently this term to ensure that she would earn the senior honor status. This is indicative of her character; she is a self-disciplined, highly motivated student. One reason that she does not have a lengthy list of school activities is that she knew that she must use much of her time studying to be able to complete her program of study and to prepare herself for college.

Susan is a pleasant young lady who is eager to help others. She has volunteered at Building Blocks Day Care assisting with the supervision of three-year-olds. She offers a friendly smile as she tutors middle school students in math and science. These experiences are beneficial to her as she prepares to become a physical therapist. She will begin her postsecondary education at East State University.

Since there are five people in Susan's family, I know that this scholarship would be very important to her and her parents. Her brother is a student at East Technical College and her sister is planning to attend there in September, 200X. I am pleased to recommend Susan for the Smith Funeral Home Scholarship.

Sincerely,

James L. Edwards

School Counselor

Martinez High School

SAMPLE LETTER 5

December 12, 200X

Dear Mr. Staples:

It is a pleasure to recommend William Miller for the Lions Club's Good Citizen Award. He is a seventh grader at Grove Middle School, and I have been his school counselor for two years.

Academically, William excels in his language arts and social studies classes. He completes all of his assignments and projects in a timely, responsible manner. After school, he tutors elementary students in reading and spelling. He greets his pupils warmly and responds to often-asked questions patiently.

William has been very active in Troop 165 of the Boy Scouts and in his church. He has participated in parades, ushered at football games, and assisted in the Thanksgiving food drive. He is friendly, self-confident, and eager to help others. I believe that he would be an excellent candidate for the Good Citizen Award.

Sincerely,

Alice Jennings,

School Counselor

Grove Middle School

References

American School Counselor Association. (2003). *The ASCA national model: A framework for school counseling programs.* Alexandria, VA: Author.

Berger, E. (1995). *Parents as partners in education: Families and schools working together.* Englewood Cliffs, NJ: Prentice Hall.

Bottoms, G., Han, L., & Presson, A. (2003). *Doing what works: Moving together on high standards for all students.* Atlanta, GA: Southern Regional Education Board.

CORD. (1999). *Tech prep: A proud choice for educational improvement—A leadership guide for counselors.* Waco, TX: Author.

Covey, S. R. (1992). *Principle-centered leadership.* New York: Simon & Schuster.

Dimmitt, C. (2003). Transforming school counseling practice through collaboration and the use of data: A study of academic failure in high school [Electronic version]. *Professional School Counseling, 6*(5), 340–350.

Feller, R. (Ed.). (1998). *Developing a career center.* Retrieved November 30, 2003, from www.wcis.uwyo.edu/

Georgia State Department of Education. (1998). *Framework for Integrating TECHnology: High School InTech.* Atlanta: Author.

Gysbers, N. C., & Henderson, R. (1994). *Developing and managing your guidance program.* Alexandria, VA: American Counseling Association.

Indiana Department of Education. (2002). *Best Practice.* Retrieved December 13, 2003, from www.doe.state.in.us/asap/bestprac1.html

Isaacs, M. L. (2003). Data-driven decision making: The engine of accountability [Electronic version]. *Professional School Counseling, 6*(4), 288–296.

Lankard, B. A. (1991). *Strategies for implementing the national career development guidelines* (Report No. EDO-CE-91-117). Columbus, OH: ERIC Clearinghouse on Adult, Career, and Vocational Education. (ERIC Document Reproduction Service No. ED338898)

Maggio, R. (2001). *How to say it.* New York: Prentice Hall.

Massey, M. S. (1998). *Promoting stress management: The role of the comprehensive school health programs.* Washington, DC: ERIC Clearinghouse on Teaching and Teacher Education. (ERIC Identifier ED421480)

Matthews, J. (2003, June 2). The 100 best high schools in America [Electronic version]. *Newsweek.* Retrieved October 24, 2003, from www.csh.k12.ny.us/highschool/data/100_best_high_schools_in_america.htm

Miller, J. V. (1991). *The national career development guidelines* (Report No. EDO-CG-92-27). Ann Arbor, MI: ERIC Clearinghouse on Counseling and Personnel Services. (ERIC Document Reproduction Service No. ED347493)

Miller, S., Wackman, S., Nunnally, E., & Miller, P. (1988). *Connecting with self and others.* Littleton, CO: Interpersonal Communication Programs.

Minke, K., & Anderson, K. (2003). Restructuring routine parent-teacher conferences: The families-school conference model. *The Elementary School Journal, 104*(1), 49–69.

Minnesota Higher Education Services Office. (n.d.). *Counselor recommendations.* Retrieved December 15, 2003, from www.mheso.state.mn.us/mPg.cfm? page ID=1029

Moles, O. (Ed.). (1996). *Reaching all families: Creating family-friendly schools.* Washington, DC: U.S. Department of Education.

Morehead, M. A. (2001). *Dealing with the anger of parents.* Retrieved January 8, 2004, from New Mexico State University Web site: http://education.nmsu.edu/ci/morehead/handouts/newangry.html

Morganett, R. S. (1990). *Skills for living: Group counseling activities for young adolescents.* Champaign, IL: Research Press.

Morrissette, P. J. (2000). School counselor well-being [Electronic version]. *Guidance & Counseling, 16,* 2–7.

Murray, R. (2002). Senior projects contribute to a strong year of challenging courses and practical experiences. *Southern Regional Education Board Update, 7,* 19–20.

The National Career Development Guidelines high school student competencies and indicators. (n.d.). Retrieved December 4, 2003, from www.cde.ca.gov/spbranch/ssp/ncdg_high.html

The National Career Development Guidelines middle/junior high school student competencies and indicators. (n.d.). Retrieved December 4, 2003, from www.cde.ca.gov/spbranch/ssp/ncdg_middle.html

Queen, J. A. (2002). *Student transitions from middle to high school: Improving achievement and creating a safer environment.* Larchmont, NY: Eye on Education.

Sabella, R. A., & Booker, B. L. (2003). Using technology to promote your guidance and counseling program among stakeholders [Electronic version]. *Professional School Counseling, 6,* 206–214.

Schutt, D. (1999). *How to plan and develop a career center.* Chicago: Ferguson.

Shea, I. M., & Bauer, A. M. (1991). *Parents and teachers of children with exceptionalities.* Needham Heights, MA: Allyn & Bacon.

Shertzer, B., & Stone, S. C. (1971). *Fundamentals of guidance* (2nd ed.). Boston: Houghton Mifflin.

Southern Regional Education Board. (2002). *High schools that work: An evidence-based design for improving the nation's schools and raising student achievement.* Atlanta, GA: Author.

Swap, S. M. (1993). *Developing home-school partnerships: From concepts to practice.* New York: Teachers College Press.

U.S. Department of Education. (2000). *Career clusters—cooperative agreements; Notice inviting applications for new awards for fiscal year 2001.* (CFDA No. 84.051B, pp. 1–13). Washington, DC: Author.

U.S. Department of Labor. (1991). *A SCANS report for America 2000: The secretary's commission on achieving necessary skills.* Retrieved December 7, 2003, from www.academicinnovations.com/report.html

U.S. Military Entrance Processing Command. (1998). *Exploring Careers: The ASVAB Workbook.* North Chicago, IL: Author.

Utah State Office of Education. (2003). *The Utah Comprehensive Guidance Program Model, 1988.* Retrieved June 13, 2003, from www.usoe.k12.ut.us/ate/compguide/history.html

Wonacott, M. E. (2001). *Career portfolios: Practice application brief no. 13.* Columbus, OH: ERIC Clearinghouse on Adult, Career, and Vocational Education. (ERIC Document Reproduction Service No. ED451345)

Index

**CORWIN
PRESS**

The Corwin Press logo—a raven striding across an open book—represents the union of courage and learning. Corwin Press is committed to improving education for all learners by publishing books and other professional development resources for those serving the field of K–12 education. By providing practical, hands-on materials, Corwin Press continues to carry out the promise of its motto: **"Helping Educators Do Their Work Better."**

The American School Counselor Association (ASCA) is a worldwide nonprofit organization based in Alexandria, Virginia. Founded in 1952, ASCA supports school counselors' efforts to help students focus on academic, personal/social, and career development so they not only achieve success in school but are prepared to lead fulfilling lives as responsible members of society. The association provides professional development, publications and other resources, research, and advocacy to more than 15,000 professional school counselors around the globe.